Words of Praise for
When the Canary Stops Singing

- Before you is a manifesto of new strategies for American business…that might save your business, or inspire it to flourish. But do not expect the ordinary. Do not expect business as usual. These authors were prepared to break with business convention in order to get at the *heart* of the matter…. Read it and allow yourself to be inspired.

  —Patricia Aburdene and **John Naisbitt,**
  partners, Megatrends, Ltd.; authors, *Megatrends,*
  Megatrends 2000, Megatrends for Women,
  and *Reinventing the Corporation*

- This marvelous volume offers far more than just new ideas—it is a life-changer. It gives readers an unforgettable tour through the future—a future these women authors have made present realities in many workplaces…. The best business book to appear in the '90s.

  —Denise Breton and **Christopher Largent,**
  authors, *The Soul of Economies:*
  Spiritual Evolution Goes to the Marketplace

- *When the Canary Stops Singing* encourages personal reflection about balancing personal and business priorities…it is provocative, insightful, and a unique business book.

  —Betsy Burton, CEO, SuperTans, Inc.,
  former CEO, Super Cuts

- Original and insightful! It is exciting to see women coming up with new models for the workplace. I have always believed we can't be two different people at work and at home. I'm glad to know that I'm not alone.

  —Gun Denhart, co-founder and CEO,
  Hanna Andersson

- The authors challenge us to explore how modern business can flourish by giving birth to vital organizations that create and nurture quality partnerships, true community, sustainable development, and whole systems thinking. These are voices which offer important practical wisdom for business leaders, no matter what gender.

  —**Juanita Brown,** president,
  Whole Systems Associates

- At long last, a business book that offers the wisdom, power, and humanity residing in the other half of the work force. This breath of fresh air really could provide the new perspectives needed to cure today's management malaise.

  —**William Halal,** professor of management,
  George Washington University,
  author, *The New Capitalism*

- In a business world dominated by men but populated by women, it is refreshing to read a book that proceeds solidly out of women's experience. This book gives voice to approaches that are fresh, inspired, informed, and honest.

  —**Diane Fassel**, coauthor,
  The Addictive Organization

- Speaks to the yearnings for congruence between economic livelihood and search for a meaningful and fulfilling lifework—for both women and men. The idea to have a group of women write about the coming change in business was inspired; the product is impressive.

  —**Willis Harman,** author, *Global Mind Change,*
  coauthor, *Creative Work*
  co-founder, World Business Academy,
  president, Institute of Noetic Sciences

- A rare perspective on organizations, management, and change—from the experience of women executives and entrepreneurs. Hopefully, their radically honest and comprehensive approaches together with their philosophical depth can instill new vision in business and provide a new benchmark in business literature.

    —**Hazel Henderson,** author,
    Paradigms in Progress and
    The Politics of the Solar Age

- Provocative and essential concepts! With unusual candor, these courageous women speak the truth about what's required to transform our organizations.

    —**Beth Jarman** and **George Land,**
    authors, *Breakpoint and Beyond,*
    and founding partners of Leadership 2000

- Terrific book! Perceptive, inspiring, and pragmatic. The authors' ideas are pertinent and fresh…emphasizing balance and integration for today's workplace while providing new perspectives for tomorrow's…unique and fascinating!

    —**Linda Morris,** director,
    Industry Services Education,
    Ernst & Young

- This book is powerful evidence of how business could lead us into a prosperous future if we all—women as well as men—integrated the male and female aspects within us. I recommend it highly to anyone seeking new visions in the world of business. Your thinking, for sure, will be provoked.

    —**Rolf Österberg**, former chairman,
    Swedish Newspapers Association,
    former CEO, Svensk Filmindustri,
    and author, *Corporate Renaissance*

- *When the Canary Stops Singing* is a "must read" for any business man or woman who wants to dance to the new music of the marketplace. It is not a book about "women's issues" but examines how work can be more meaningful to the whole human being—male or female.

  —**John Renesch**, publisher,
  The New Leaders newsletter,
  editor, *New Traditions in Business:
  Spirit & Leadership in the 21st Century*

- What a great idea! This collection gets into issues that we all realize are essential but normally avoid or deny..... It takes us from a clear look at the tragedies of today's machine-age management to the glories possible when we use all of our aspects and create a present and future with respect for the earth and all living things.

  Be prepared to be shocked, excited, pleased, uplifted, and led to a realization about what needs to be done and how to do it.

  —**Michael Ray,** professor,
  Stanford Business School,
  coauthor, *Creativity in Business*,
  coeditor, *The New Paradigm in Business*

- If there is a deeper promise to women in the workplace it lies in creating a current of change in deep assumptions and habitual ways of acting and being with one another. This book explores that promise as well as any I have read. You cannot read chapter after chapter without beginning to appreciate the profoundness of the changes that lie ahead if we truly begin to realize our potential for working creatively together.

  —**Peter Senge,** author,
  The Fifth Discipline,
  Director of Systems Thinking, MIT

When The Canary Stops Singing

When The Canary Stops Singing

Women's Perspectives on Transforming Business

Edited by Pat Barrentine

Authors

Riane Eisler • Carol Frenier • Kathleen Keating

Marie Kerpan • Barbara Shipka

Kim McMillen • Jacqueline Haessly • Jan Nickerson

Anne L. Rarich • Jeanne Borei

Hope Xaviermineo • Cheryl Harrison

Mitani D'Antien • Barbara Fittipaldi • Sabina Spencer

Berrett-Koehler Publishers
San Francisco

Berrett-Koehler Publishers, Inc.
155 Montgomery St.
San Francisco, CA 94104-4109
Tel: 415-288-0260   Fax: 415-362-2512

Ordering Information
Individual sales. Berrett-Koehler publications are available through most bookstores. They can also be ordered direct from Berrett-Koehler at the address above.

Quantity sales. Special discounts are available on quantity purchases by corporations, associations, and others. For details, contact the "Special Sales Department" at the Berrett-Koehler address above.

Orders for college textbook/course adoption use. Please contact Berrett-Koehler Publishers at the address above.

Orders by U.S. trade bookstores and wholesalers. Please contact Publishers Group West, P.O. Box 8843, Emeryville, CA 94662: 510-658-3453; 1-800-788-3123.

Printed in the United States of America

Printed on acid-free and recycled paper that meets the strictest state and U.S. guidelines for recycled paper (50 percent recycled waste, including 10 percent postconsumer waste).

Library of Congress Cataloging-in-Publication Data
When the canary stops singing: women's perspectives on transforming business / edited by Pat Barrentine / authors, Jeanne Borei... [et al.].
     p.   cm.
   Includes bibliographical references and index.
   ISBN 1-881052-41-9
   1. Women in business.   I. Barrentine, Pat. II. Borei, Jeanne.

HD6054.W48 1993   93-27145
331.4'—dc20   CIP

First Edition
First Printing 1993

This book was conceived and produced by New Leaders Press, producers and hardcover publishers of *New Traditions in Business: Spirit & Leadership in the 21st Century* (John Renesch, editor). Electronic publishing by Barrentine Associates.

Cover Design: Michael Rogondino

*This book is dedicated to the men
and women throughout the world
who are contributing to a
transformation in business practices
so as to provide for sustainable growth,
social responsibility, and the nurturing
of the human spirit.*

Table of Contents

Acknowledgments

The authors wish to thank John Renesch, the founder of New Leaders Press, who conceived of the idea for this collection and invited them to contribute. They also want to acknowledge Pat Barrentine for her commitment, skill, and patience during the editing, design, and production process for this book. Linda Alber, who served as project coordinator for this collection is also the recipient of the authors' gratitude.

In particular, Sabina Spencer thanks her partner John Adams, for his wonderful loving support. She also thanks Amy and Guy Tolhurst who, as children, offer so generously the gifts of beauty and wisdom. To Peter Russell and Sharon Lehrer, she offers thanks for the many explorations into realms unbounded by time and space.

Hope Xaviermineo wishes to publicly acknowledge Willis Harman for being her teacher and mentor. She also thanks her sister Joy Mineo and her mother Beverly Goldman for their unconditional love, Dona Nassar for helping her in her writing, and her husband Tom for his support in her life and being the most gentle soul she has ever known.

Jan Nickerson gratefully acknowledges Rondalyn Whitney and Sydney Rice for their committed coaching, Wynne Miller and Janet Britcher for helping her hold a vision and their suggestions regarding early drafts, and Mary Jane Nickerson and John Graham for their undauntable support and belief in her. For their grounded inspiration she thanks Rondalyn, Sydney, Wynne, Jeanne McConnell, and Joan Sweeney.

Cheryl Harrison acknowledges Michael Wright "inside out and backwards," Terry Oldano for being her creative counterpart, Jerry Jacob, Bill Perell, Lonnie Zwerin, and Shelli Winter for their support, their encouragement, and their wisdom.

Barbara Shipka thanks Peter Krembs and Charlaine Tolkin for their spiritual, intellectual, emotional and financial support on this project as well as over the decades. She also acknowledges Kazimierz Gozdz, Faith Ralston, and A.B. Reynolds for their encouragement, input, and critique of the many drafts of her chapter. A special thanks to John Renesch for his vision in conceiving of this book and his willingness to trust that those of us who are not well-known writers have something of value to share.

Jacqueline Haessly thanks Sabina Spencer who encouraged her to participate in this book. She also thanks Dr. Robert Pavlik, Robert Weisenborn, Dr. Pravim Kamdar, and Robert Aubrecht for their time and support over the years, helping her focus the language of peacemaking in a manner that speaks to the business community.

Carol Frenier acknowledges the "Village Virgins" for their listening and encouragement, Patricia Stimpson, Sydney Rice, and Juli Ann Reynolds for their dialogue in which the specific idea for her chapter began to take form, and from which the title of this book evolved.

Kathleen Keating wishes to acknowledge mentor and co-gardner Robert deVito, as well as Stephen Roulac for his untiring late night editing assistance.

John Renesch acknowledges the advisory board for Sterling & Stone, Inc. for their year-round support. The advisory board consists of Pat Barrentine, David Berenson, M.D., William Halal, Ph.D., Willis Harman, Ph.D., Paul Hwoschinsky, James Liebig, William Miller, Shirley Nelson, Christine Oster, James O'Toole, Ph.D., Steven Piersanti, Michael Ray, Ph.D., Stephen E. Roulac, Ph.D., Jeremy Tarcher, Margaret R. O'Keeffe Umanzio, and Dennis White.

Much gratitude is due to intern André van Regenmortel, a Dutch student who helped us with this book.

Editor Pat Barrentine thanks John Renesch for inviting her to participate in this project, Steve Piersanti of Berrett-Koehler for his encouragement and support of her writing, and Patty Mote Lacey for her skill in copyediting. She also thanks her children Marcia, Alan, and Lee—her friends and teachers—for their support, and especially her husband Gene, who died in January of 1993, for his undying love and encouragement of her personal and professional growth for over forty-two years.

Special thanks are also due to those individuals who generously reviewed the complete collection in manuscript form and offered comments that could be included as advance praise for this book. In addition to those previously acknowledged, they include Denise Breton and Christopher Largent, Juanita Brown, Betsy Burton, Gun Denhart, Diane Fassel, Hazel Henderson, George Land and Beth Jarman, Linda Morris, Rolf Österberg, and Peter Senge.

To our friends at Berrett-Koehler Publishers, Inc., we owe much gratitude. To founder-publisher Steven Piersanti, director of marketing Patricia Anderson, production director Elizabeth Swenson, and cover designer Michael Rogondino as well as staff members Mark Carstens, Valerie Barth, Lis Paulus, Kristen Scheel, Stephen Zink, Valeria McOuat, and the team at Publishers Group West.

With particular gratitude, we acknowledge Patricia Aburdene and John Naisbitt, authors of *Megatrends 2000* and *Megatrends for Women,* for writing the Foreword and for their personal commitment to the values expressed in these pages.

Patricia Aburdene and **John Naisbitt** are the world's leading social forecasters. Their decade-long literary collaboration has produced three major books on trends, transformation, and change, with a combined in-print figure of 14 million copies worldwide. *Megatrends 2000* (1990) has been published in thirty-two countries and was a best-seller in the United States, Japan, and Germany. *Megatrends* (1982) was on the *New York Times* best-seller list for two years. *Re-inventing the Corporation* (1985) has been published in a dozen countries.

Patricia Aburdene has lectured extensively throughout the world on the impact of social and economic change on business and society and the future of the corporation. John Naisbitt, an advisor to many of the world's leading corporations and heads of state, has thirty years of business experience, both as a successful entrepreneur and as an executive.

Patricia and John are married and live in Telluride, Colorado and Cambridge, Massachusetts, and maintain an office in Washington, D. C.

Foreword

Patricia Aburdene and John Naisbitt

Before you is a manifesto of new strategies for American business. The women who contributed to this book are like researchers who have carefully documented their experiments and painstakingly crafted their conclusions, but who now enthusiastically race out of the laboratory to share their exciting news with us. Their field, however, is not science but business. Their findings might save your business, or inspire it to flourish.

But do not expect the ordinary. Do not expect business as usual. These authors were prepared to break with business convention in order to get at the *heart* of the matter.

Though some might object to our characterizing their complex journeys in this way, we think the following questions thematically link each fascinating contribution:

- What is wrong with business today?
- Why is the environment in most businesses today so inhospitable to vital, alive human beings?
- How does one change it?

To answer these questions, especially the last, the authors have drawn on their feelings, emotions, intuition, empathy, awe, and faith—the very core of their spiritual beings. Furthermore, they have integrated their deeply held values into the workplace.

Guess what? They got results which were as practical, as concrete, as you will find in any "self-help" book. They solved problems, streamlined procedures, increased productivity, generated sales and profits, and created a new, far more humanistic success story.

It is critical that what these women learned in the hot houses of pure experimentation be made available to American business at large.

In early 1993, IBM announced a $5 billion loss, the largest in U.S. business history. Fortunately for IBM, the firm did not hold that questionable distinction for long. A week or so later, Ford Motor Company reported a $7 billion 1992 loss, again the biggest in U.S. business history. But the very next day, Ford's name was pushed out of the headlines by an astounding announcement from General Motors—the auto giant had lost a gargantuan $23 billion in 1992!

It would not be difficult to conclude that American business is in crisis. But is it?

The following statistic suggests something else: *Women-owned businesses employ more people than all of the companies in the Fortune 500 combined.*

What does this mean? We believe it means that in the United States, two separate and distinct commercial "realities" exist side by side in two very different states of economic viability. One thriving; one in decline.

Women-owned businesses are the fastest growing sector of small to mid-size businesses, which represent the lion's share of the U.S. economy. The Fortune 500 constitute only about 10 percent of the U.S. GDP. Women-owned businesses, lean and mean—not only because women have so consistently been denied access to capital to expand, but because they run their businesses in a very conservative manner—are hiring new people all the time.

In addition, the ranks of women-owned businesses swell each year with thousands of talented, competent women, who were passed over for promotion. It's called the "glass ceiling." These women declare "The heck with this," start their own firms, taking an average of 35 percent of their former clients with them.

The old centralized, male-dominated bureaucracies that have been around for years are indeed at a crisis point. In the past decade, the Fortune 500 have collectively laid off an average of 200,000 to 300,000 people a year.

Big, it seems, is not beautiful, not these days. Not in business. And, "bigness" is not the only problem in business today.

The Industrial Corporation

In *Megatrends 2000* we wrote, "Corporations as we have known them were created by men for men. After World War II, America's fighting men exchanged their military uniforms for factory overalls and gray flannel suits." The authoritarian, military approach to organization—which had guided men so well in warfare—now became the management model by which they would run their companies in peace time. It actually worked quite well for about three decades.

But change, dramatic change, the enemy of the status quo, emerged in time. The U.S. shifted from an industrial to an information economy. Foreign competition forced American business to seek new markets in the world economy. And women, millions and millions of them, without backgrounds in the military model of management, flooded the U. S. work force.

Now, in an information-based economy where people are well educated, where people are expected to think for themselves, and to manage themselves, leadership cannot be defined according to the military model—that is "issuing orders."

Leadership must inspire people to be committed to a company's vision and values. It must "bring out" the best in people: supporting them, encouraging them and, perhaps most importantly, giving them the authority they need in order to carry out the shared corporate vision. *Many of the business leaders who are doing that best today are women.*

In *Megatrends for Women* we wrote, "In a time of change and crisis, women became leaders of small and mid-sized firms. With no background in sports or the military, the business metaphors of the industrial age, and few mentors to teach them the masculine ways, women were thrown back on their instincts.

"Some authors had advised women to imitate 'male' strategies, but the old ways didn't work for *anyone,* and no one knew how to manage under the new circumstance."

In the past twelve years, we have addressed four books to corporate audiences and have always believed that business was more willing to change, to adjust to new circumstances than most other institutions. Failure to do so simply costs too much money.

But our faith in business has been shaken in the past year or so and we feel *more* resistance to the new ideas that women and sharp younger male managers bring to the party. That resistance, we believe, is not unrelated to the record financial losses described earlier.

While women and young male leaders want to empower people—they relish the flexibility of networking structures—older male leaders who have worked in hierarchies all their lives often resist innovation. They continue to place time-honored faith in the status quo and, perhaps more importantly, in the values and structures that brought them to power, even though they know intellectually that these values do not hold the importance they once did.

Hierarchies are unbelievably slow to change; they favor conformity and the status quo. Hierarchies generate hugely unwarranted confidence in their ability to survive despite changing exterior conditions.

4

IBM was and, despite its valiant efforts at restructuring, remains a centralized bureaucracy. It is a victim of its own metaphor: the mainframe computer—big, centralized, and irreplaceable. It's a company of the whiz-bang information age encrusted in the party costume of an industrial dinosaur, too confident of the status quo, too big to move even in the face of the stunning new machine created by those two young men in that California garage.

For decades, the Big Three auto makers have known what consumers liked about foreign cars and that customers want to conserve energy. Did they change their product, invest in people and plant? That is a rhetorical question, indeed. Instead, buoyed by the special privilege of a huge domestic market, they acted, until very recently, as if they had a manifest destiny to go on forever.

Five years ago the big U.S. car companies possessed the marketing resources to figure out that 50 percent of the cars were sold to women. Yet they still used women as sex objects to sell cars to men. Hello?

What was happening in these hierarchies? The suggestions for change that came up from the ranks from smart young engineers, marketing executives, and creative directors, were squashed at the top because "we have always done it this way."

When Roger Smith, former CEO of General Motors retired, corporate guru Peter Drucker publicly suggested that the person who should replace him was Frances Hesselbein, former head of the Girl Scouts. Drucker pointed out that she had a track record in turning around a huge bureaucracy—exactly what General Motors desperately needed at the time. Hesselbein also had mastered what she called the "web style of management," a circular approach to the corporate organization chart which breaks down hierarchies and speeds up the flow of information.

G.M. opted to ignore Drucker's suggestion, promoted someone from within, and proceeded to lose the $23 billion. Maybe next time they will listen.

The authors of this book are entrepreneurs, consultants, corporate women, and thinkers of all stripes. Their voices echo those of women business owners and of corporate women creating change in the Fortune 500 and elsewhere in corporate America.

While big companies conduct "business as usual," the women who contributed to this book are pioneering innovation. They offer painful struggles, striking new metaphors, stories and legends, fresh analogies: the corporate mythology of tomorrow, the raw, vital stuff of transformation, real and yet unfolding still.

Read it and learn.

Read it and allow yourself to be inspired.

Read it and then start your own experiments.

—Patricia Aburdene and John Naisbitt
September 1993

Pat Barrentine is a free-lance writer and owner of Barrentine Associates, an information packaging and communications company. Her business career has included owning retail and consulting businesses, free-lance public relations and marketing. She was a founding team member of the World Business Academy, an international network of businesspeople who recognize a personal commitment to the creation of a positive future for the planet. She was editor of *World Business Academy Perspectives*, a quarterly journal, until June, 1993.

She served on the founding board of the Peninsula Conservation Center, and was named Conservationist of the Year for 1970 by the Loma Prieta Chapter of the Sierra Club. Other board service has included organizations involved in spiritual growth, conflict resolution, and political action. In 1987 she was honored as Member of the Year by the Northern California Chapter of the National Speakers Association. She serves on the advisory board for Sterling & Stone, Inc./New Leaders Press and the editorial board for the World Business Academy.

Introduction

Women as Harbingers of Business Transformation

Pat Barrentine

The title for this book evolved from a discussion among Carol Frenier and three female business associates. They were trying to understand the frustration each of them felt working in the corporate environment. Many of their friends and co-workers were experiencing similar difficulties. It occurred to them that perhaps women were to business what the canary once was to the coal miners—when the canary stopped singing, it was a warning that the environment was too toxic for living creatures. Perhaps women in business are harbingers of a needed transformation.

According to Webster, a harbinger is "one who presages or foreshadows what is to come." If women are business's early warning system, and many of them find the workplace inhospitable, stifling, and toxic, what needs to happen? The authors of this book offer us some new ways of doing business. They open our minds to new ideas and viewpoints.

This "toxic" environment doesn't affect only women. Many of the concerns expressed by women are shared by an increasing number of men. Both men and women who hold prestigious positions in large corporations are leaving to start their own businesses or to join smaller, entrepreneurial groups. But not everyone has the luxury of being able to leave, nor would that be healthy for business. Men, perhaps, are the least free due to their obligations to support a family, although the freedom to change jobs or professions is an increasing concern for many women. The challenge for business is to create more humane and nurturing workplaces for everyone.

As I talked with some of the authors of this book, it became clear that it was the *feeling* they had in the corporate environment that became intolerable. Some felt they were being asked to become a person they didn't want to be.

In "Love at Work," Carol Frenier relates that when she didn't feel comfortable doing business the "right" way—being tough, watching people, withholding information—she thought *she* was the problem. I feel that her response is fairly typical of women—certainly it has been my pattern. If something didn't *feel* right, it was probably just because *I* didn't understand. Other authors echo that sentiment, saying that self-reflection is a common attribute that women share. When Carol shifted to her natural nurturing and supportive attitude toward her employees and clients, her comfort level, and her success, increased.

All the authors of this book are women, and the new way of doing business that they present is a feminine way—feminine as Carl Jung defined the term, in that the characteristics of loving, nurturing, and compassion do not belong to women alone.

The essays connect at the level of feeling—love, truth, authenticity, and nourishment of the human spirit. The authors speak of balance and personal responsibility. Work becomes an arena for self-discovery. The metaphors they use are organic—life returning to the pond, gardening—in contrast to more traditional male metaphors taken from sports and the military.

Trust and a willingness to risk are evident in these essays, as is a search for personal and spiritual freedom. The authors look to the self—the individual, not the system—for solutions. Their way of doing business empowers individuals and recognizes their value—their sacredness, if you will.

In the variety of their writings, we find many similarities in what they consider important, in their decision-making styles, and in the way they value and nurture relationships. The stories they share are personal—the authors risk telling the truth, and that's what makes them valuable. This is a book about the value of connection, spiritual development, authenticity, and truth in business.

Why are these values important to the future of business? Like all institutions, business organizations can fall into the trap of unconsciously perpetuating the status quo unless someone questions accepted "truths." If the old way works, that's great. But we all know that most businesses are in trouble today, largely because of their inability to change old patterns. In their own way, women are challenging that way of doing business— not just for themselves, but for everyone.

As executive Marie Kerpan points out, many women bring a "healthy disrespect for the status quo" into the workplace. Some things do need to change. For example, I can't help but reflect on the experience of my oldest son who once worked in a printing company that posted the names of the employees responsible for making errors. If you messed up, everybody in the shop knew it. Needless to say, that tactic did little to improve morale, productivity, or quality. Notice the difference in the story Mitani D'Antien tells about the woman manager who had her group share their "wins" at weekly staff meetings. This group improved performance as they focused on success rather than failure. Employees thrive when they experience success and feel fairly treated and appreciated.

Women have a strong need for authenticity—and being authentic means being *all* of yourself. Society has encouraged workers to "leave their *selves* at the door." Of course, outside pressures and responsibilities come through the door with everyone anyway, but, those in the predominantly hierarchical work force have learned to put on the "proper" business demeanor and shut out the rest of their lives while on the job. Focus on work is certainly called for. However, what is out of balance is that feelings have not been welcome in the work setting.

It hasn't necessarily been easy for some women to enter the work world. A Big Six executive told me, "The challenge of switching from being home with children, which requires absolute trust, candor, and love, to an environment where people work from hidden agendas, goals aren't communicated, and emotion is considered 'ungrounded' was a shock. The first week of work, I cried every night when I got home."

Interdependence and the Organic Metaphor

There is a shift taking place in business. Riane Eisler, best-selling author of *The Chalice & the Blade* (Harper & Row, 1987), identifies it as a shift from the *dominator* style—"power over," conquest, control—to the *partnership* model—"power to," life giving, life nurturing. She believes that the large number of women entering the workplace has been a major influence in this shift. She sees tremendous human costs imposed on both men and women by the hierarchical, authoritarian system that is "all too often abusive and dehumanizing." She traces the history of early societies in which women played a more central role, where women were not excluded from positions of leadership. These societies were generally more peaceful, she says.

Eisler emphasizes that "while women today can make a special contribution to the creation of a more productive, creative, and humane workplace, this in no way means that men do not also have a very important role to play in the process." She identifies steps for creating a full and productive partnership between men and women—a necessary component in the economic and cultural shift we must accomplish.

Carol Frenier's discussion with women friends who were questioning their role in business led to a greater understanding of the "toxicity" in the workplace and led to the title of this book. She talks about love at work in a way that gives us a new understanding of the value of being free to express feelings.

The workplace is changing, and new values are gaining support. Flexibility is required to accommodate the physical and emotional needs of single parents—both men and women. It's hard for workers to concentrate on business if they don't feel that their children are safe and well cared for.

In "Organizational Gardening," Kathleen Keating says she has learned that she can't expect her associates to operate in isolation from their many important roles outside their organization any more than her garden is free from influences from neighboring properties. She goes so far as to state that "a business that is insensitive to its associates' family roles is destined to fall far short of what it might achieve." She compares the symbiotic relationship between plants in her garden with that of people in her organization and notes the necessity to give both plants and people a nourishing environment in which to thrive. To produce such an environment, she carefully balances her role, both in her garden and in her business, as visionary, coordinator, and "doer." The importance of maintaining a balance among all areas of one's life is a concept stressed by several of our authors.

Balance, Harmony, and Nurturing the Spirit

Balance is a recurring theme in this collection—balance between personal needs and work responsibility, between family and job, between outside obligations and time for oneself, and between the needs of the business and those of the community. Marie Kerpan believes that one aspect of this balancing is "the need to temper the race for wealth and power with the higher values of a civilized society, such as integrity, prudence, compassion, and authenticity."

Balance includes time for our spiritual development as well. Until quite recently, it was most unusual—even suspect— to include the concept of spirituality in a business book. This is partly a holdover from our commitment to "separation of church and state." But it's more than that. Our "spiritual life"—whether that means religious pursuits or a personal quest—has been considered as "separate from" the rest of our lives. These authors suggest something quite different, and some even go so far as to recommend a recognition of spiritual values in the workplace. They share an orientation toward life characterized by a personal commitment to self-discovery, transformation, and spiritual growth.

Barbara Shipka shares how much she learned about herself during the three years she spent working in Somalia and other impoverished areas of the world. When she returned to her corporate consulting practice, her experience helped her recognize the "spiritual poverty" she found in business. She talks about spiritual poverty as a hunger of the soul that can be as devastating as physical hunger if less obvious. "In corporations, fear, anxiety, a sense of isolation, apathy, and despair are the results of spiritual poverty, and their effects on us are similar to the disease, starvation, and death in refugee camps." Barbara reminds us that spiritual poverty robs us of our creativity, sense of meaning, and joy in our work.

However foreign the subject of spirituality may be in most businesses, it is clear that increasing numbers of people are seeking spiritual meaning in their lives. For some, opening themselves up spiritually can provoke a crisis—an "inner" crisis that is not always understood even by the person it's happening to. Pointing to her own personal experience, Kim McMillen cautions that a person going through an "awakening" may find it difficult to function fully on the job. She challenges business organizations to support the personal integration of their employees by creating a "spiritual haven" in the workplace.

Spiritual development is as yet unfamiliar to many of us because it is so personal that many people don't discuss their experiences—especially with fellow workers. Hopefully, the time will come when the counseling and support needed in this area will be as accepted as psychological counseling is today.

The search for personal integration and meaning naturally leads to a concern for the environment in which we live at home and at work—for our global community. Women will continue to play an important role in creating a more positive future on this planet. For the most part, we have an aversion to war and other practices destructive to other humans and all living things. Making a difference requires a commitment to work wherever we are, with the tools we have developed, and to take responsibility for our actions. Jacqueline Haessly suggests six values for the global marketplace: ecological balance, social responsibility, political participation, economic transformation, global spirituality, and a world without armed conflict. She speaks of economics as the "management of goods and services for our global household." Running a household in most parts of the world is still "women's work." Those of us working in business as well have an opportunity to bring a more balanced ecological consciousness into the workplace.

Creating Networks, Support Systems, and a Spirit of Community

Self-discovery used to be something almost no one talked about—certainly not with people at work. The current proliferation of "support" groups is an indicator of the need many have for connection with others who have shared similar experiences. There are several ways in which we can support and nourish each other through life's myriad changes. Support groups focused on a disease, a psychological trauma, or grief tend to be something that people come to for as long as needed and then move on from. On the other hand, networks, while they may change with time and with changing circumstances, are more lasting—often enduring for many years. For example, my network includes people who don't necessarily know each other, yet each of them is available for specific kinds of support or advice. In business, many of us create or join networks through which we can share ideas and information, especially when free from the rigid constraints of a hierarchical system.

Jan Nickerson reports a productive use of networks in her essay "Helping Your Dream Job Find You." She tells us about the support networks she developed and used in her job search. Not only did these contacts help her, but she was able to pass along leads that she couldn't use (or that didn't fit her vision) to others. Her multigenerational family (a special kind of network) was a major part of her support team.

Jan uses the gardening metaphor to describe the stages of her job search. "I had seen others go into any garden and pick whatever was blooming, often the first flower they saw," she says, "often without apparent regard for whether it was a weed, an annual, or a perennial." Sometimes people get panicky when out of work and reach out for any opportunity rather than following a well-thought-out plan. Jan carefully "planted" only those job opportunities she wished to "bloom" in her garden and prepared the "soil" with care. When harvest time came, her garden bloomed beyond her expectations.

Networks tend to proliferate in times of transition—times when people feel a strong need to connect with each other and find the truth for themselves. When major change is taking place in our personal lives or our work, having a group to meet with to discuss possibilities and offer mutual support can mean the difference between lapsing into paralyzing fear and moving forward constructively. Fortune 100 executive Anne Rarich was able to create support networks in her organization to help co-workers deal with the threat of and, later, the effects of "downsizing." Many of these groups were made up solely of women who "found safety in these core groups to explore their concerns." The healing atmosphere they provided for each other was critical and the overwhelming response to the opportunity should provide a model for other companies contemplating the same process.

The networks I'm speaking of are quite different from the "old boys' networks" that both women and men have felt excluded from. The new networks include nurturing and sharing. They are built on mutual support, not granting of special favors or notice. They are expansive, not exclusive—they can include men *and* women, people of all races, those at different levels in a company or positions in a community.

The need to connect at a deeper level, to have more authentic relationships and clear communication, motivates most women. The experience of this new way of connecting with friends, family, or co-workers is often referred to as a feeling of "community." In contrast to a network, which is naturally fluid, a "community" has implications for continuity, lasting connection, and deep purpose. Community sometimes happens spontaneously, but having the process directed by a trained facilitator can be most useful.

In "From Chaos to Community," corporate executive Jeanne Borei shares a profound experience she had in a "community-building" workshop. Community-building is a concept put forth by best-selling author Dr. M. Scott Peck in *The Different Drum* (Simon & Schuster, Inc., 1987). As a result of her experience, Jeanne recommended that her entire organization undertake the process. Explaining why they would enter such a process, she says, "We were headed toward an inevitable day of reckoning. We didn't know it until it was on top of us." To embark on even the first step was a risk—reaching community is not guaranteed. But she saw the potential and was willing to take the risk. The rest of the management team agreed. The entire company has benefited from her courage and inspiration, and every employee has now gone through the community-building process. Jeanne's organization is the only one using this process that has made the total commitment of involving all its employees. Without Jeanne's commitment to creating an open process, the transformation they have experienced would never have happened.

I was able to observe two of the authors of this book in a group setting where their training in community-building was profoundly evident. They each communicated their feelings in a manner that was clear, honest, and direct. Their communications generally started with "I feel…." Staying in touch with feelings is an important part of community-building and fosters authentic relationships and open communication.

In sharing her vision of "A World We've Only Dreamed Of," Hope Xaviermineo says that the place to begin creating a better world is with ourselves. Having successfully brought to fruition a vision of good health for herself following a devastat-

17

ing accident that left her paralyzed, she challenges us all to join in holding a vision of a "perfect" world. Aspects of her vision include "a business environment... where people play, learn, and work together in the deepest and purest sense," "each individual's internal growth is recognized as his or her primary purpose," and "the higher good has priority, and out of that we all prosper."

Openness, Intuition, and the Process of Change

Recognizing the needs of employees to grow as people creates an environment in which, as Hope says, "everyone prospers." Entrepreneur Cheryl Harrison increased her firm's productivity by sharing information and responsibility for the outcome with all her employees. She found that when she trusted people to come up with good solutions, they needed her less, experienced more personal success and, therefore, took more responsibility for results. "We work very collaboratively in the office to prepare for a client presentation so that everyone really knows what's going on. If the baton needs to be passed... everybody's very comfortable doing that." She finds that the collaborative spirit of working out a problem together is heightened when nobody has to report to anyone. "People are responsible for themselves."

That style of management takes a lot of trust on the part of a business owner. Learning to trust oneself is necessary before one can trust others. One way to develop that kind of trust is by developing of the intuition.

"Intuition can enhance decision making and managerial strategy," says Mitani D'Antien. She relates the story of a client who was able to trust herself to take a bold stand in a business situation by trusting her intuition. Intuition—fortunately no longer referred to as "*women's* intuition"—is increasingly accepted as a decision-making tool in business. It's been interesting to see the openness of many men who now freely admit to using intuition to make decisions. While it is uncertain how much influence the increasing number of women in the workplace has had in stimulating that comfort, something has changed. Mitani calls intuition "an invaluable key to unlocking future successes." As we continue to ride the waves of change, it's important to be able to trust our inner knowing and our ability to make clear decisions. Intuition is tuning in to that inner knowing—it's listening for clues.

Listening—inner and outer—is a skill that these authors employ to maintain clarity in communications. The ability to *really* listen makes a profound difference in our personal effectiveness. I recently had some experiences in a book study group where we experimented with several exercises involving communication. Each of us was surprised to find how difficult it was at times just to *listen* rather than getting ready to answer the person who was speaking as soon as he or she finished. I learned even more by reading Barbara Fittipaldi's essay on listening. Her finely developed sense of the way in which communications miss the mark because of inadequate listening skills increased my level of awareness. To listen effectively, I have to be willing and able to hear the feelings behind the words being said. How often we take for granted unexamined and unspoken assumptions about "what is." We simply assume we know the "truth" without looking to discover where our thought patterns and beliefs originated and whether or not they are still useful, or actually true.

Any progress toward a more perfect world will require a different kind of leadership. Sabina Spencer says the new form of leadership is "more a state of consciousness than a set of skills or traits." In "Seven Keys to Conscious Leadership," she says, "Such a leadership consciousness recognizes the tremendous interdependency that exists not only among the departments of an organization but among nations of the world." She finds conscious leadership "planted firmly in the earth...its source is 'divine' inspiration." Noting that the changes required will take "courage, commitment, and the belief that it is both possible and desirable for such a profound transformation to occur," she reminds us that "we live on the edge of our own discovery."

19

The edge of our own discovery can be a pretty lonely place. A friend who works for a major corporation recently told me that, as a new employee, she was confused after strategy meetings. Being not only new, but the only woman in the room, she observed the men presenting the pros and cons of a situation and, with little discussion, making a decision. When questions occurred to her—usually after they had finished the business at hand—she decided she must just be slow or must just not understand. As she worked there longer, she found out that the men didn't understand any better than she did—they just didn't dare to admit it. Her company has since created new forms of meetings, including the use of brainstorming techniques. "We are much more process oriented now," she says. Did her questioning of the old way make a difference? I believe it did.

That willingness to be "out there" and share what is real doesn't come easily. It takes personal courage and conviction to be open and vulnerable, especially in a business setting.

How Women Make a Difference

A recent members' meeting of the World Business Academy was, for me, a fascinating demonstration of the differences between men's and women's perspectives on the role of business in their lives. The theme of the meeting was Courage in the Workplace. Gail Thomas, founder of the Dallas Institute of Humanities and Culture, set the stage. She explained that the way the divine gets to "play" in the world is through spirit. Our relationship with spirit is our soul. "Courage," Gail says, "is our ability to trust spirit to work in the world through us." The old paradigm myth of courage for men, she told us, is Prometheus, chained to a rock, vultures eating away at his liver. The new paradigm myth of male courage is Hermes, the God of Commerce, who crosses boundaries, establishes relationships, and links the gods with humanity.

Following this presentation, those men who had been invited to share their personal stories spoke. While their stories were very real, their approach tended to be more mental, objective, and linear. Clearly, they had met major challenges and taken risks in business, but we heard little personal history—the stories were about their role in business.

In exploring feminine courage, Gail explained, "Spirit wants to get away and become unencumbered by form. Our life goal is to learn how to hold or ensoul spirit." Courage for women is symbolized by the myth of Demeter (earth mother) and her daughter Persephone, the soul who slips into the underworld of not knowing to gain access to imagination. The feminine way is to join with others and trust the unknown.

We experienced a supreme example of feminine power in the sharing that followed. When the women told stories of their businesses, they shared from their hearts and souls. The stories were personal, frequently starting with childhood, family—the life experiences that had led them to find their place in the business world. All the women had experienced major success in business, many of them as single parents. I heard no blaming men for any struggles they had experienced. I heard compassion for themselves and others—laughter mixed with pain. It was a beautiful example of feminine power—not "power over" others or circumstance, but a deep sense of personal discovery and achievement.

A tremendous sense of empathy developed between the men and the women in the room. When it was time for lunch we all hesitated. Everyone seemed to want to maintain the connection that had been created. Several of the men had tears in their eyes. Said one, "I've never heard anything like this before." It is difficult to put into words the emotional impact those women had by sharing in a business group at that level of feeling and truth, but I know that everyone in the room was changed.

After you have read this book, I suspect that you will also be changed.

Pat Barrentine, editor

Part One

Interdependence and the Organic Metaphor

Women, Men, and Management:
Redesigning Our Future
Riane Eisler

Love at Work
Carol Frenier

Organizational Gardening : A Metaphor
for the New Business Paradigm
Kathleen Keating

This part focuses on nurturing, caring, and respect for individuality. Riane Eisler speaks about the need to nurture and respect the contribution women make in the workplace and examines the masculine and feminine as social constructs that vary depending on whether they are in the context of what she calls a partnership or a dominator model of organization.

Carol Frenier writes about "love"—a term usually not associated with a discussion of business. She says that "even writing the word *love* makes me wince, because it is overworked and misunderstood and because there is such danger that it will be read sentimentally." She believes we thwart our own nature when we work in an environment where we feel no deep connection to the people with whom we work. Part of the massive change that the business community is being asked to make is to recognize and accept *feelings* in the workplace. "Love at Work" will open your eyes—and heart—to new possibilities in business.

Kathleen Keating draws knowledge and learning from her experiences as a gardener and business executive, seeing the parallels between the needs of plants and the needs of people. Those needs touch what most of us deeply value—recognition of who we are, being in an atmosphere where we can "flower," and being surrounded by compatible people.

The authors in this first part, as well as many of the others, stress the need to recognize our growing interdependence as well as the organic nature of life in organizations.

Riane Eisler is the author of the international bestseller *The Chalice & The Blade: Our History, Our Future,* hailed by Ashley Montagu as "the most important book since Darwin's *Origin of Species.*" She is also coauthor, with social psychologist David Loye, of *The Partnership Way: New Tools for Living and Learning.* She is co-founder of the Center for Partnership Studies, has taught at the University of California and Immaculate Heart College, and has published many books and articles, including *The Equal Rights Handbook* and contributions to *The World Encyclopedia of Peace, The Human Rights Quarterly, Behavioral Science,* and *Futures.* She is also a fellow of the World Business Academy.

This essay is based on a paper she authored for the tenth annual congress of the Finnish Society for Futures Studies and the Turku School of Economics. It is excerpted from an article in the January/February 1991 issue of *Futures,* an international journal based in Great Britain.

1

Women, Men, and Management: Redesigning Our Future

Riane Eisler

All around us, the world—including the workplace—is in flux. There is growing recognition that fundamental changes are needed for economic and perhaps even species and planetary survival.

The crisis of centrally planned Soviet and Eastern bloc economies has dramatically highlighted the ineffectiveness of a top-down economic architecture wherein workers are seen as cogs in a giant machine. In "free-market" economies such as that of the United States, economic problems have also spurred a search for new ways of structuring the workplace through more lateral (team) work modes, more people-centered (nurturing) leadership styles that support greater creativity and productivity, and attention to issues such as flextime, child care, and other benefits that take into account the whole of people's lives, outside as well as inside the workplace. At the same time, first on the bottom rungs, and then trickling up into middle and occasionally top management, women have entered the paid labor force in unprecedented numbers.

Is the simultaneity of these changes merely coincidental? Or is there a relationship between them, which in turn reflects even more fundamental but still largely unexplored systems dynamics? This essay examines these questions—and their implications for the workplace and society at large—from the new perspective of two underlying types of social organization introduced in my book *The Chalice & The Blade* (Eisler 1987): the dominator and partnership models. Specifically, it places important contemporary economic trends as well as changes in gender roles and gender-related values in the context of a movement toward fundamental social and ideological change. Moreover, it looks at these issues—particularly the issue of women as managers or leaders—in the even larger context of our cultural and social evolution.

Women, Men, Work, and Power

In the conventional frame of reference, the terms *woman manager, woman leader,* and *woman executive,* are in themselves anomalies. In our history books, empresses such as Catherine the Great and, more recently, presidents such as Corazon Aquino have by and large stepped into positions of leadership as the widows, daughters, or mothers of men. In business, too, management has been a male preserve, with the occasional top executive who is a woman figuratively stepping into the shoes of men. In other words, power has been practically synonymous with maleness. And it has, by and large, been equated with a particular type of power (the power to give orders and to be obeyed) and with certain types of characteristics (such as strength, toughness, and decisiveness) stereotypically considered masculine. In sum, power has generally been depicted as power over people and, even more specifically, as a male's power to control people (be it for ill or good).

That view of power is highly appropriate for a social organization that orders human relations primarily in terms of ranking—man over man, man over woman, nation over nation, and man over nature. And it is instructive to remember that, not so long ago, this kind of rank ordering was said to be divinely ordained, be it the "divine right" of a king to rule over his

28

"subjects" or the right of a male "head of household" to rule over his wife and children in the "castle of his home."

Economic relations in this model of society were also believed to naturally follow this pattern. Just as women's and children's labor was by law and custom the property of the male head of household, the labor of slaves (and later, to a large degree, of serfs) was said to be due their owners or lords. Even later, in the early stages of the Industrial Revolution, with the shift from a primarily agrarian to a manufacturing economy, the relations of workers and bosses tended to follow this mold. Sweatshops, where women, men, and children worked from dawn to dusk in unsafe and oppressive conditions, were accepted as "just the way things are." And the use of force by industrialists against those who sought to organize workers was often condoned and at times backed up by government leaders.

Indeed, whole societies were basically held together by fear backed by force, reinforced by ideologies that commanded loyalty, fealty, and obedience to orders from above—from God (as in the admonition that we must be God-fearing), from kings and lords, from male heads of households, and, in more recent times, from employers (bosses), be they business owners or managers. It was thus the role of the manager, whether as foreman or top executive, to increase production through rewards and punishments designed to maintain vertical hierarchies in an economic system where either monopolies or dog-eat-dog competition were the norm, where women were relegated to the lower-pay and lower-status jobs, and where caring and empathy were seen as having little, if any, relevance.

There were, of course, also lateral relations, bonds based primarily on trust and caring, as without these society could not have functioned. But while the value of these informal relations was often extolled, what counted in actual practice was one's position in the more formal vertical structures—familial, social, and economic. And while there were kings, lords, heads of household, and later industrialists and managers who were noted for their caring and empathy, these were by and large the exceptions to the norm.

29

If we now look at two of the major trends in the workplace today—the movement of women into leadership levels and the movement by many women and men toward more empathic or nurturing management styles—we see that both are fundamental violations of earlier norms. And we also begin to see that these trends are not unconnected; that, on the contrary, when viewed from a systems perspective, they are inextricably intertwined. For what they challenge are basic assumptions, not only about the roles of women and men but about the nature of work and power.

We are not used to making these kinds of connections, because we have been so conditioned to view anything connected with women or femininity as peripheral, unimportant, and clearly secondary to what transpires in the "real" or "men's" world. But a very different perspective emerges once we take a closer look at some of the contemporary changes in the workplace from a gender-holistic perspective—one that gives equal value to both the female and male halves of humanity.

What we are dealing with here is not a question of women against men or men against women. Rather, it is a question of social organization. What have been described until now are ways of looking at women, men, work, and power that by and large conform to what I have termed a dominator model of society—a way of structuring human relations where, beginning with the ranking of one-half of humanity over the other, the primary organizing principle is ranking, of men over women, men over men, nation over nation, man over nature, or employer over employee.

The terms *masculinity* and *femininity* as used herein (and as still generally used) are to a large extent constructs appropriate for a dominator rather than a partnership model of society. For this is a system where men are socialized for domination and conquest. Moreover, what we are dealing with is *not* a matter of simple linear causes and effects. Rather, it is a matter of systems dynamics. In other words, we are dealing with complex interactions among mutually supporting and interwoven systems elements—interactions on which an examination of the hitherto

30

neglected but socially fundamental organization of gender relations sheds important new light.

Dominator and Partnership Models

In my work over the past decades, I have been reexamining human society from a perspective that takes into account the whole of our history (including our prehistory) and the whole of humanity (both its female and its male halves). As I used this larger data base, what became increasingly apparent was that underneath the great surface diversity of human society, transcending such differences as time, place, technological development, ethnic origin, and religious orientation, are certain basic patterns or configurations that are characteristic of the two models of social organization that I have been mentioning, one oriented primarily toward domination and the other toward partnership.

For example, societies that are conventionally viewed as very different—Khomeini's Iran, Hitler's Germany, Stalin's U.S.S.R., and the Masai of nineteenth- and early-twentieth-century Africa—all have striking similarities. They are characterized by rigid male dominance, a generally hierarchical and authoritarian social structure, and a high degree of institutionalized violence (that is, a fear/force-based mode of internal as well as external relations). They are also societies where so-called masculine values, such as toughness, strength, conquest, and domination, are given high social and economic priority (as in the emphasis on weaponry) and so-called feminine values, such as caring, compassion, empathy, and nonviolence are, along with women, generally relegated to a secondary or subservient sphere that is cut off from the "real world" of politics and economics. Finally, this is a model where difference (whether based on sex, race, tribal or ethnic origin, religion, or belief system) is equated with inferiority or superiority and where in-group versus out-group thinking and behavior are the norm. This is part of the configuration characteristic of societies that are oriented primarily toward what I have called the dominator model.

The Dominator and the Partnership Models: Basic Configurations		
Component	**Dominator model**	**Partnership model**
One: Gender relations	The ranking of the male over the female, as well as the higher valuing of the traits and social values stereotypically associated with "masculinity" rather than "femininity"	Equal valuing of the sexes as well as of "femininity" and "masculinity," or a sexually equalitarian social and ideological structure, where "feminine" values can gain operational primacy
Two: Violence	A high degree of institutionalized social violence and abuse, ranging from wife- and child-beating, rape, and warfare to psychological abuse by "superiors" in the family, the workplace, and society at large	A low degree of social violence, with violence and abuse not structural components of the system
Three: Social structure	A predominantly hierarchic and authoritarian social organization, with the degree of authoritarianism and hierarchism roughly corresponding to the degree of male dominance	A more generally equalitarian social structure, with difference (be it based on sex, race, religion, or belief system) not automatically associated with superior or inferior social and or economic status

By contrast, in the partnership model of society, difference—beginning with the most fundamental difference in our species, that between women and men—is valued (as in the ideal of the more pluralistic society now gaining currency). In this type of social organization, whether the family, the workplace, or society at large, so-called feminine qualities and behaviors are not only held in high esteem but incorporated into the operational guidance system, particularly in more "soft" or empowering rather than "strongman" or disempowering leadership styles. And here there is also a generally more equal partnership between women and men, less institutionalized violence, and a more democratic or egalitarian social structure.

Once again, this configuration transcends the conventional differences in time, place, level of technological development, and so forth. For example, while there are technologically primitive tribal societies, such as the BaMbuti, !Kung, and Tiruray, that are oriented toward the partnership model, we also see strong trends in this direction in many modern industrial nations, particularly in the Scandinavian countries. In Finland, Sweden, and Norway, for example, we see that attempts to

32

create a more equitable economic system resulted not, as they did in the U.S.S.R., in a dominator form of communism ruled from the top but rather in a democratic society with a mix of "free enterprise" and "the welfare state." And here we also see a strong interest in nonviolent means of conflict resolution (for example, the creation of the first peace academies) as well as systemic attempts to create a more gender-balanced society— one where women, along with "feminine values," are no longer relegated to an inferior status and excluded from the "real" or "public" world.

Moreover, there is mounting evidence that this type of social organization is not, as is commonly believed, a modern invention. Rather, thanks to what British archaeologist James Mellaart (1965) calls a "veritable revolution in archaeology," data are accumulating indicating that this way of structuring society has very ancient roots. In prehistoric societies, it appears to have flourished for thousands of years in the mainstream of Western cultural evolution before the shift, during a period of chaos and cultural bifurcation, to a world oriented primarily toward a dominator system of "strongman" rule.

All this takes us back full circle to the subject of women, men, work, and power. The way that these earlier, more partner-ship-oriented societies conceptualized power was very differ-ent from the way that we have been taught to see it. In these societies, the powers that govern the universe were not seen as a male deity whose symbol of authority is a thunderbolt (Jeho-vah or Wotan) or a weapon (Zeus or Thor). Rather, their concep-tion of power focused on the power to give, sustain, nurture, and illuminate life, symbolized since remote antiquity by the female figure of a Great Goddess from whose womb all life ensues and to whose womb it returns at death, like the cycles of vegetation, to be reborn again. In other words, here the highest power was seen not as "power over" (domination, conquest and control) but as "power to" (life-giving and life-nurturing).

There is also evidence that in this earlier way of structuring society (which goes back to circa 7000 B.C. in the European Neolithic and could still be found in the Minoan civilizations of

33

Crete until circa 1200 B.C.), women were not excluded from positions of leadership. Women were priestesses, and from Minoan society we find images, such as the so-called procession fresco, indicating that the position of high priestess was central to the functioning of society.

Moreover, these seem to have been more generally peaceful societies than we see today. While they were not ideal societies and undoubtedly experienced some violence, they do not seem to have glorified violence as "heroic" or "manly" or institutionalized it through practices such as rape and warfare, which are absent in their extensive art.

Another interesting characteristic of Minoan civilization was its extraordinary creativity and inventiveness. Its beautifully alive and naturalistic art has been described by scholars as unique in the annals of civilization. And this creativity seems to have spilled over into its technology and business life. Here we find the first paved roads, viaducts, and even indoor plumbing in Europe. And, as Platon writes in *Crete*, Minoan civilization had a remarkably high general standard of living, with extensive public works. Not surprisingly, the Minoans were also the great trading people of their time, with trade routes extending as far as Egypt.

I suggest that this information and the new view that it offers of our prehistory are of relevance to much that is happening in our time. They confirm something that we are beginning to understand better from many contemporary sources—that a dominator model of social organization is less creative and productive than one oriented more toward partnership, be it through less expenditure for warfare or more teamwork and worker involvement. I also suggest that the contemporary re-emergence of a "softer" or, in terms of dominator stereotypes, more "feminine" style of leadership and governing ethos, particularly in the world of business and economics, can be better understood in the larger context of a fundamental social and ideological transformation, the shift toward a partnership way of structuring society.

These prehistoric data also shed important light on the urgency of this shift, at a time when the dominator ethos of conquest and domination threatens all life on our planet. In terms of this larger perspective, we can see that the problem is not, as sometimes argued, advanced technology but the potentially lethal mix of high technology with a dominator ethos of conquest and domination—"man's conquest of nature"—particularly in a time of mounting environmental crises. And we can also begin to see that in both human and economic terms the dominator model is wasteful and inefficient, with its chronic weapons expenditure drain (which, as armaments become more technologically complex and expensive, threatens even the most affluent nations with bankruptcy), its emphasis on coercion, and its suppression of creativity and the expression of people's need for meaning and connection with others through their work.

Toward a Redesigned Workplace

Viewed from this more holistic perspective, we can see how the construction of the modern workplace was in critical ways patterned to conform to the requirements of a dominator rather than a partnership type of social organization. Not only was it to be generally hierarchical and authoritarian; it was also primarily designed by and for men who were, in turn, programmed to maintain this type of system.

The human costs to both men and women of this imbalanced, fear-based, institutionally insensitive, and all too often abusive and dehumanizing way of organizing and managing business and to the social and economic structure that it reflected were enormous. But it was said, and generally believed, to be a necessary requisite for economic productivity.

As Clement L. Russo (1984, 1985) writes in his article "Productivity Overview: Recognizing the Human Dimension," what is emerging is a new view of the workplace as a partnership-oriented structure that can "transform the 'daily humiliations' of work into an activity that gives meaning, direction, and self-fulfillment" and that provides "the opportunity to cooperate with others in a common enterprise that stimulates respect, creativity, and commitment that will ultimately benefit everyone."

That this design will indeed "ultimately benefit everyone" is also being increasingly shown in practice. For example, as early as the 1960s at a Volvo plant in Sweden, workers' teams were organized that met together and decided how they wanted to divide their jobs, when to stop and start the assembly lines, and even what hours to work. The result was both far higher productivity and a much lower number of defects. Similarly, in an article called "Creating a New Company Culture," Brian Dumaine (1990) reports that in DuPont's plant in Towanda, Pennsylvania, where managers call themselves "facilitators, not bosses," productivity has increased by a huge 35 percent over the past four years. And what makes this plant different and so exceptionally productive? It is once again "organized in self-directed work teams, where employees find their own solutions to problems, set their own schedules, and even have a say in hiring."

This is an important move toward a new corporate culture, one that, to paraphrase DuPont's CEO, Ed Woolard, promotes the creation of more effective "partnerships" to better serve four interrelated constituencies—the customer, the employee, the shareholder, and society at large. It is a culture that recognizes the cultural importance of human beings and human relations. And it requires a fundamental shift in leadership and management styles. As Woolard puts it in his interview with *Fortune* on the subject of corporate restructuring, "the first thing people watch is the kind of people you promote. Are you promoting team builders who spend time on relationships, or those who are autocratic?" (Dumaine 1990).

In short, what we are told by a growing number of organizational development experts as well as corporate CEOs is that what is urgently needed for both the economy and society is a fundamentally redesigned workplace, one that nurtures human development and promotes cooperative rather than hierarchical human relations. And integral to this redesigned workplace

36

is what we may call a partnership rather than a dominator style of management, emphasizing worker motivation rather than coercion.

Gender Issues and the Restructuring Process

Until now, most books and management training programs that prescribe decentralized structures, participatory teamwork rather than top-down chains of command, nurturing rather than coercive management styles, and "win-win" rather than "win-lose" approaches have only implicitly, rather than explicitly, related these shifts to changes in gender stereotypes or gender-linked values—much less to anything that has to do with the socioeconomic status of women. But these systems connections are increasingly becoming explicit, as women from all over the world examine their situation in the larger context of a dominator model of society.

The problem, however, is that if women are forced to operate in dominator-style structures, they are under tremendous external and internal pressure to "be more like men." As noted by Alice Sargent and Ronald Stupak (1989) in *The Androgynous Manager*, women—particularly as middle managers, but sometimes even when they reach the top—will have to "step into the shoes of men" (as was the case in earlier dominator structures and has been said of Margaret Thatcher, who, perhaps unfairly, has been referred to as "the best man in England").

On the other hand, there is mounting evidence that in situations where women have a strong voice in shaping the system's rewards and incentives, the culture and structure of the workplace are fundamentally altered. In *The Female Advantage: Women's Ways of Leadership*, Sally Helgesen (1990) describes the innovative organizational structures and strategies of a number of successful women managers. She documents how the workplaces run by these women tend to be more like "webs of inclusion" than hierarchies of exclusion, to be communities where sharing information is key. And she also points out that this structure has the advantage of permitting a greater flow of information, because there are more points of connection or contact than in a hierarchy, where the information flow is strictly up or down along appropriate channels.

Managers of the Future

Once again, it is important here to emphasize that while women today can make a special contribution to the creation of a more productive, creative, and humane workplace, this in no way means that men do not also have a very important role to play in the process. The military (dominator) model that has been the norm for structuring the workplace has been disempowering to both women and men. And it will require women and men working in full and equal partnership to transform that model.

It is also important to emphasize that today many men (even CEOs of major corporations) are rejecting dominator approaches and moving toward a more "feminine" or nurturing way of managing and organizing business. But viewed from a systems perspective, these changes in male attitudes and behaviors are not happening in a vacuum.

If men are finding it possible to adopt more "feminine" values and behaviors, it is in part because the status of women and, with it, men's attitudes toward what is "feminine" and "masculine" are changing. An example is the current trend toward men redefining their role of fathering to include some of the nurturing behaviors stereotypically associated with mothering. This trend is not unrelated to the movement toward more "feminine" or nurturing management styles for both men and women. For as women and the "feminine" rise in status, men can increasingly respect—and adopt—"feminine" attitudes and behaviors.

Moreover, it is important to emphasize that while some traits defined as "masculine" in dominator structures (conquest, domination, and the suppression of empathy and caring, along with "effeminate" aesthetic sensibility) have stunted men's full human potential, other qualities that are also considered "masculine," such as decisiveness, assertiveness, risk taking, and so forth, are in fact valuable in a structure oriented primarily toward partnership rather than domination.

An ethos of "corporate caretaking" shared by both women and men is clearly a key element in the transformation from a dominator to a partnership business culture. But since this ethos of "corporate caretaking" in essence stems from what in dominator societies is considered a "feminine ethos," this transformation cannot take root unless there are also fundamental redefinitions of stereotypical gender roles, both "masculine" and "feminine."

A striking example of such a management partnership—and a fitting ending for this essay—is the extraordinarily successful partnership of Anita and Gordon Roddick, whose company, The Body Shop, has become a model for the socially and ecologically conscious corporation of the future. What The Body Shop sells, in Anita Roddick's words, is not only "sound products" (ecologically sound health and beauty aids) but "sound values" (from human rights and ecological consciousness to the promise of a humanized workplace). Anita and Gordon's joint aim is to "rewrite the book of business," to "be committed to social responsibility, global responsibility," and "to empower their employees." And largely through Anita's exuberant, often flamboyant, and always unconventional approach to business (which includes a studied irreverence toward the "old boys" and their ways of operating), and both Anita and Gordon's commitment to a "feminine ethos" of corporate—indeed, global—caretaking, The Body Shop has in a few years grown into a multinational, multimillion-dollar business, as well as an important force for positive social change.

Conclusion

I have focused on the interconnection between access to economic and social policy-making and management roles for substantial numbers of women and the shift from what I have called a dominator to a partnership model of society. Unlike most of what has been written on the entry of women into higher management, my focus has not been on the all too familiar problem of women's difficulties breaking through what is commonly called the invisible "glass ceiling" built into most business and other organizations, which excludes the female half of humanity. Rather, it has been on the organizational architecture itself—not only its gendered glass ceiling but its totality, including its social and cultural foundations.

What I am proposing is that this architecture needs to be redesigned and that women can make a critical contribution in this regard. I am also suggesting that the presence of women in policy-making and managerial positions is a necessary, though not sufficient, precondition to the economic and cultural shift from what I have called a dominator to a partnership-oriented society—and that this transformation requires that careful attention be paid to hitherto ignored gender issues.

Finally, I believe that this transformation is urgently needed at a time when the stereotypically "masculine" leadership and management styles, as well as the dominator hierarchies that they help to maintain, are proving incapable of dealing with our mounting economic, social and ecological problems. And I am convinced that, at this time of rapid and potentially destructive technological and social change, only a full and equal partnership between women and men, informed by an ethos of caring, can ensure that the partnership movement that we are seeing in both the workplace and society at large will succeed.

Carol Frenier is president and co-owner of The Advantage Group, Inc., an advertising and marketing company serving dairy corporations in the United States. She graduated from Brown University in 1966 with a bachelor's degree in American history. She taught high school social studies for nine years and received a master's degree from Goddard College in women's studies before entering business. She is a student of Jungian depth psychology and has participated in dream analysis for two years.

She has been married to Bob Frenier for twenty-three years. In addition to sharing a business, they have shared many other activities, such as Beyond War (now the Foundation for Global Community) and the study of gender differences. Most recently, they moved to rural Vermont to live more simply in the natural world.

2

Love at Work

Carol Frenier

Once, for almost a year, I spent two days a week with a female colleague, Colquitt Meacham, trying to figure out where we had lost our footing in the public sector. Colquitt, a lawyer by training and the first woman dean of a respectable New England college, and I, a partner with my husband in an advertising firm, were on the verge of permanently dropping out of business life as we knew it. We felt a deep sadness and a strong sense that we were on to something that was fundamental to our lives. We read copiously that year, mostly Jungian depth psychology, and then came together and tried to draw out of each other our deepest feelings about our public lives.

When I look back at the pages of material we assembled, what stands out for me is that we felt that there was a central part of ourselves that was left at the door when we entered corporate America. Naming that part would be difficult. It was like a ball of mercury rolling around on the bathroom floor, with us down on our hands and knees trying first to catch it and then to hold on to it.

What we were trying so hard to identify was really very simple, but it was hard to acknowledge. *There is general agreement among scholars that the human species has an inherent drive to develop consciousness, that is, according to Webster, to gain an ever increasing "awareness of one's own existence."* I have come to think that there is also in human beings a drive toward love that is as strong as our drive toward consciousness. But even writing the word *love* makes me wince, because it is so overworked and misunderstood and because there is such danger that it will be read sentimentally. Everywhere people are trying to connect, to love, but much of it is awkward and bland and without substance. There is much talk about love, but when you look closely at what is actually occurring, it doesn't seem to amount to much.

I am not talking about some superficial touchy-feely experience (though that is often a sincere effort to get at love). Think, for a moment, of the last experience you had when you came upon a beautiful vista. Such an experience is always unexpected, even when you are consciously seeking it. When a place is particularly beautiful to you, it literally takes your breath away. What you experience in that moment is awe. You can feel the experience in your body. The response, the intense *feeling* response, is more than just sensing a connection to the beauty or to the whole. It is a profound and active *engagement* with it, a loving of it from the center of your soul. That is what makes you weep.

That powerful emotion is what I am talking about as the "drive toward love." It seems to me that it is instinctual in us to feel that strongly. It is involuntary. We do not *decide* to love the beauty. We just do. It is the emotion that blows us away, not the beauty per se.

That may seem obvious, but I think we are more uncomfortable with this drive toward love than we know. We label it "obvious," then run away from it; that is, we run away from doing any deeper work with it. How does it work, and what can it produce? We expect to have to learn to read, to do math, or to build a house, but we are not comfortable learning about the range of feelings that we possess. There is no body of practices (outside of therapy, which to many implies dysfunction) for helping human beings differentiate their feelings and use them to generate rather than to destroy. Mastery in this area often seems like controlling our emotions, including the best of them. We are almost universally embarrassed when we are publicly moved to tears. We apologize.

Feelings and Business

This is even more pronounced in business. I would say that this drive toward love, in its most mature and adult form, is given little if any room to evolve in our business lives. There are endless courses and trainings to help us to be more effective in the workplace, but few of them focus on how to evoke and fine tune our most deeply held values. The closest we can get to this is to extol enthusiasm and excellence, but we still feel compelled to justify these in terms of their positive impact on the *bottom line*. Presumably, otherwise, they would not be important.

As I look back on my work life, particularly in the prerecession 1980s, when my company had a staff of ten people, this drive showed up in me as a kind of fierce, even blind commitment to the people who worked for me and even to the people in other companies with whom I worked. My feelings were regularly bruised by the behavior expected of me in the name of being an effective businessperson: withholding the whole truth to avoid being taken advantage of, asking for more than I wanted or offering less than I was willing to give so there would be more room to negotiate, making hard and fast rules for employees on the grounds that I could get "softer" later, but couldn't get "tougher." All these things made a certain logical sense, but they never did feel right.

Because I was convinced that it was "me" that was the problem, it never occurred to me to simply throw out the rules, experiment my own way, and see what happened. There was one exception, from my earlier days as a teacher. I discovered that if I told my students the truth about what I felt and needed, they were perfectly capable of responding to me as a human being. Out went the rule about being tough first, soft later!

I tried to act consistently with what I believed in my mind was true. Of course, I was never wholly successful in preventing the undercurrent of what I felt was undermining me. For example, I got regularly "caught up" in my employees' lives, in their daily successes and defeats, no matter how hard I tried to be "objective." The peaks in my business life almost always involved a "team" success, not just for the results we produced, but for the camaraderie of doing it together.

Underneath, I had a nagging suspicion that this enthusiasm for the team was "soft" and too "mothering" and not good for people or the business in the long run. Yet one of my most satisfying moments occurred when a board member showed up early, hung around the office for a while, and then mentioned to my partner that he was beginning to see what kind of ambience I had created in the office. He couldn't name it, but he could *feel* it. As I recall this incident, I am reminded of reading Max DePree's *Leadership Is an Art* (1987). I felt myself inexplicably moved to tears at every page. It is just now occurring to me that I could feel in his writing the atmosphere that he created in his company by his deep love, and I was so starved for love in business that it made me weep.

I also took a secret satisfaction in the absolute success of three young women in my employ, Marylou Black, Elaine Sutherland, and Ro Watson, to resist any and all attempts to put them into an organizational chart. No matter how many times we reconfigured and reassigned "accountability," they always said, "Sure," and went right back to what they were doing. While I know it wasn't that simple from their point of view, it looked effortless and miraculous to me. Each one of them had a primary area of responsibility; without any direction from management, they also learned enough about each other's job to take over in a pinch. They anticipated that there would be periods of overload for each of them and that each other's strengths, weaknesses and fluctuation of energy levels would be part and parcel of the daily routine. Like a river, they were inseparable and organic, and no one could improve on their model.

Intuitively they knew, as all of us know, that we thwart our own nature when we work in an environment where we feel no deep connection to the people with whom we work. When experiencing emotion strong enough to make us weep is taboo, or when all of our private relationships, enthusiasms, sorrows, and crises are split off from what we do for eight to ten hours a day, we feel alienated from ourselves.

It pains me to recall the times when I was consistent with what I thought I *should* do at the expense of what I felt at a deeper level. I often overruled my gut values and initiated or enforced policies that I now deeply regret. For long periods of time, I even believed my own rhetoric. For almost a year, we employed a sales manager who swamped my staff with work of questionable value and made endless demands on their time. I condoned this behavior on the grounds that others knew more than I did about what was needed. At the time, *excellence* was the buzzword in all the business literature. To question the necessity of producing reams of paper, or to want to leave the office at a reasonable hour to be with your family at home, was viewed as laziness and lack of ambition.

In a recent conversation with other women in business, I found the same feeling of regret about yielding to the views and decisions of others. Gradually, these women had realized that others did not necessarily know more than they did, but they had trouble taking their own observations seriously. It is hard to do that when there is not yet a useful body of distinctions and practices to which we can refer when we are making judgments from our values rather than from knowledge.

The emerging acceptance of intuition helps; it validates the idea that a "gut feeling" can be as on target as hard scientific data. But our gut feeling often has to do with what we value, as well as an inner way of knowing. "It doesn't feel right" can mean "It's not correct," or it can mean "I don't feel good about it; it is not the right thing to do." My experience is that many business men and women who are exploring the uses of intuition mean the latter as often as they mean the former, but it is not a technically correct use of the term as I understand it. In any case,

I sense that this concept of valuing is sufficiently misunderstood to merit a totally separate consideration.

Many men share the experience of not trusting their own judgment, but what I do not hear from them as often as from women is a second phase of realization that what they know literally cannot be heard at this time. Several men have asked me to say more about what that "knowing" is, but it is still very much like the ball of mercury to me, elusive and vague.

While we may draw the same ethical conclusions, there is good evidence that men and women arrive at these conclusions differently, using different data. Carol Gilligan's *In a Different Voice* (1982) offers a provocative view on this. Essentially, she says that male moral development focuses on principles of reciprocity and fairness, while female moral development focuses on one's responsibility within an existing web of relationship. In other words, it is an issue of principles versus the needs of individuals within unique situations. A male colleague of mine, who is a product manager in a large corporation, pointed out to me that this difference may be more a product of Western culture than of inherent differences between men and women, as evidenced by the more relationship-based Japanese business style. So the reason this difference between men and women showed up in Gilligan's research may be because in our culture, women are less rigidly trained than men, rather than because of anything inherent about gender.

Whatever the reason, this difference was a revelation to me. I started to notice that I went through two processes to make every business decision. First, I considered what I felt was the right relationship between the parties given their individual needs. Second, I translated these feelings into principles that could be understood in the business world. I had, of course, been doing this all during my career, but unconsciously.

The most powerful example that I can think of occurred when my business was in such economic difficulty that I had to consider breaking my lease in an expensive office building. The strategy of my male colleagues was to extract ourselves first, then negotiate a "fair" settlement with the landlord. My approach was that I first had to know what the landlord's circumstances were and whether my action would contribute to his financial demise. Once it was clear that he was in better financial shape than I was, I could consider breaking the lease. I honestly would have preferred, however, to sit down with him, look at both of our situations together, and formulate the best strategy for meeting our needs, splitting our losses, if you will, as well as our gains. Such a move in today's business environment could have left me at a substantial disadvantage. Yet time after time, when problems arose between my clients and the radio and television stations that carried their advertising, that is precisely what the female account executives and I would do.

For a long time, I secretly advocated a change from "male rules" to "female rules" as the path to greater enlightenment. As I became more at home with my own intrinsic standards, however, I could be more accepting of the "other." I also remembered that Gilligan (1982) pointed out that both genders integrate some of the other's frame of reference as they become more mature in their moral development, even if they do get there by very different paths. It seems to me now that the trick is to recognize which or what combination of "rules" apply in a given situation. I suspect that in work as well as sexual encounters, the dynamic interaction of the two is what is optimal. Life is created from the difference, not the sameness.

Finding room for the integrity of each path to be fully expressed may be more critical for the long-term health of our planet than we know. When we think of the development of consciousness, the focus of the human species for at least the past two thousand years in the Western world, we largely associate this "consciousness" with the archetypal (not gender specific) masculine, the powers of the mind and will, often symbolized by the "light" in the darkness. Many writers are now suggesting that we may have gone as far as we can go in the development of consciousness without bringing our feeling function up to the same evolutionary level as our mental or thinking function.

49

Carl Jung (1971) distinguished the "feeling" function from the "thinking" function in this way: Thinking involves ideation and conceptual connection; feeling involves valuation, that is, acceptance or rejection (and I would add enthusiasm, giving priority to, and avoidance). Thinking and feeling work together, but they are fundamentally different psychic functions, just as tasting and smelling are two distinct senses. The capacity to value is less cerebral; it is often accompanied by but is not limited to emotion.

Think, if you will, of all the language that we have for the *thinking* function: *logic, analysis, induction, deduction, planning, strategizing, calculating, conceptualizing, synthesizing,* and so forth. Now try to think of nouns that differentiate aspects of the feeling function with the same positive ambience and orientation towards results.

An example of the predominance of using our thinking rather than our feeling function in business is our preoccupation with who is at fault when something goes wrong. Recently, I was the middleman responsible for managing a client's delivery of a service to his customer. My client made a major error that resulted in a significant loss to his customer. I was alerted to the problem and went to work on finding out where the error had occurred. When I found it, I alerted the senior management, because I could see that there was a major communication gap down the line. The senior management, I felt, could break the bottleneck by presenting the "big" picture to the two parties who were miscommunicating. In my conversation with the senior manager, he was preoccupied with apologizing and focused on his resolve to find out who was at fault. What I needed, instead, was an intervention. In other words, I needed him to "teach" what he knew so that the two people could work together more effectively. Who was at fault was of no consequence to me, in fact, it did not seem to me that *anyone* was at fault. It was a meaningless question in terms of getting the problem solved.

When the feeling function is in play, there is room for this kind of intervention, because there are both expectation of and respect for the many nuances of individual perception and experience. When we are engaging exclusively with the thinking function, we are trying to determine what is objectively accurate. In the domain of the feeling function, *all* the feelings in a situation can be "right," because we are dealing with our internal subjective response.

There are at least two ways to deal with people when things go wrong. Analyzing and establishing blame is one; getting at the root of the conflicting perceptions and feelings, expressing them, and then *responding* is another. Responsibility, or *the ability to respond*, it seems to me, comes from that grounded inner feeling of genuine concern more often than from having the right idea. In truth, they work together; the best ideas are often evoked when concern is most deeply felt.

When employees anticipate being blamed, they become preoccupied with covering themselves and coming up with a good argument for why they were not at fault (and someone else was), or a knee-jerk admission of fault so that they do not appear to be unable to accept criticism. This is a far cry from the genuine feeling of regret that one's error caused difficulty or loss for another.

If we could all operate masterfully at the level of genuine concern, then what Teilhard De Chardin said years ago might become true. He wrote, "The day will come, after harnessing space, the winds, the tides, and gravitation, we shall harness for God the energies of love. And, on that day, for the second time in the history of the world, we shall have discovered fire" (Gallagher 1988).

Now *mastery* is the key word here. Each step in the struggle to evolve consciousness has been demanding and intense and has required great patience. We should expect no less in our efforts to take our feeling function to a higher level; that is, to evolve what I am calling our drive to love. We will need to make room for those with the best gifts in this area to lead us. It will not just be a matter of "deciding" to love or being "swept away." We sell this attribute short if we think of it

51

sentimentally. It will take practice to reach mastery. Its realization will be measured more in the quality of community, human and planetary, than in personal ecstasy.

Part of our struggle will be dealing with some deep fears about our capacity to love, perhaps because of its shear strength. Although nothing makes me feel so real as being inundated by such a feeling, it is also quite terrible. Will it literally tear me apart? And where there is strong emotion, there is potential for strong feelings of all kinds.

We may also be afraid that love will drown our consciousness. In his memoirs, Carl Jung (1961) describes his trip to Africa, in which he was enchanted by the strong psychic connections that the native people had with their physical environment and their tribe. But he also felt that immersing himself in this "participation mystique" would have been a step backward in his development, that is, in the individuation process of his autonomous self. He warned against it. His view reflects a common theme in Western Judeo-Christian thinking: the idea that the hard-won (archetypally masculine) consciousness will be overwhelmed and engulfed by a more primitive (archetypally feminine) symbiosis.

The word *symbiosis*, often loosely associated with relationship per se, carries with it a connotation of psychological immaturity. Autonomy has traditionally been viewed as the higher state of development. Yet, as they relate in their book *Women's Growth in Connection* (Jordan and others 1991), the Stone Center scholars at Wellesley College found that many of the women whom they studied achieved psychological maturity "in relationship." Further, they found that many women experienced empathic and intellectual responses simultaneously, not sequentially. Another way of saying this is that empathy, or merging with the feeling of another, can occur simultaneously with remembering and maintaining one's personal boundaries. Traditional psychological theory suggests that one must detach from the feeling state in order to do the cognitive boundary thinking.

If it turns out that women have a gift for integrating the two functions—for whatever reason, social training or innate psychological makeup—then they have an important role to play in our immediate future. As painful as it is to experience, there could be great potential power in sensing so keenly that something vital is lost when we feel pressed, either by external standards or by our own self-judgment, to leave so much of our drive toward love at the door when we walk into the business world. While it is not totally new, I assert that this sensing, by both women and men, is occurring on an unprecedented scale in our time.

A group of women in Boston started meeting together after a business retreat because we felt drawn to share our experiences with each other. As the months went by, we came to an idea that I think could have important implications. It occurred to us that women may be to business what the canary was to the coal miners. When the canary stopped singing, it was an early warning signal that the environment was getting too toxic for all living creatures. As women at high levels leave corporations, we might do well to find out why.

I believe that, as businesspeople and as a species, we need to start patiently, yet actively, listening to our own apparently messy, chaotic, unsystematic, and often vague gut feelings when looking at a situation that will affect people or the planet in some way. This is truly the work of love right now: to define itself and evolve a body of distinctions and practices that will allow us to put our love to work.

Kathleen E. Keating is president and chief operating officer of Axion Design, a strategic consulting firm specializing in brand identity development and consumer retail packaging. Since 1973, she has been instrumental in building Axion into a leading company in the global design market. Among the prominent international organizations for which Keating has provided creative services are Coca-Cola Foods, Nestlé, Ralston Purina, General Mills, Quaker Oats, S&W Fine Foods, McCormick/Shilling, Microsoft, and The Clorox Company.

Recognized for outstanding graphic communications work by the Western Art Directors Club, the Package Design Council, and the American Institute of Graphic Arts, Keating has received both silver and gold awards from the Packaging Association of Canada. Her award-winning package design and brand identity programs have been featured in publications such as *The Best U.S. & International Label Design, Creativity, World Trademarks and Logotypes, American Corporate Identity, Graphis,* and the annuals of The Printing Industries of America.

3

Organizational Gardening: A Metaphor for the New Business Paradigm

Kathleen E. Keating

The remnants of what had once been a lovely garden covering a residential lot were a major reason why I selected the home that I bought back in the mid-1970s. Besides all the usual reasons for buying a house, the opportunity to design, install, and care for my own garden was a powerful motivator. As a single woman in my early twenties, I was faced with a number of challenges that I would encounter again some years later as a woman assuming a senior management position in a competitive business long dominated by men.

The Metaphor

Looking back nearly two decades, I am struck by the parallels between what initially attracted me to gardening and what currently attracts me to management. Anyone who has ever assumed the responsibility for a garden of any consequence knows well the necessity of balancing hard work with a delicate touch. I have found that maintaining a vital environment for creative professionals likewise requires hard work and sensitivity, since the work that we do blends innovation with sustained effort.

Increasingly, "thought leaders" in business management are talking of a transformation, a *shift in global consciousness*, that is intended to redefine the world community, the regional communities that make up the world community, and the many public and private organizations that in turn make up various other associations. The proponents of this new paradigm assert that relationships between groups will be characterized by cooperation rather than competition, resulting in a society where the feminine *yin* perspective, rather than being subordinated, will gain equal status with the male *yang* orientation. But in my view, if a new business paradigm is to be introduced, the promised transformation will be enhanced to the extent that it embraces some of the lessons I have learned from my home gardening—from the long hours spent preparing the soil, sowing the seeds, nursing seedlings to life, and continually caring for the plants to facilitate growth to their full potential. A similar process describes my role in "gardening" my organization. Indeed, in many ways, organizational gardening is a metaphor for the new business paradigm.

I remember hearing some years ago a prevalent management practice described as "the mushroom theory" of dealing with people, basically involving keeping people in the dark and feeding them "manure." This seemed to be a common joke to describe how too many managements related to their organizations. I know there have been times when I've been so busy that I did not take the time to connect personally with my associates, and what time I did spend may have been poor quality.

In my garden, when I fail to recognize the individuality of a particular plant, the results are disappointing. Plants that need sunshine and water wilt when given darkness and fertilizer. Managements that elect to apply to the whole organizational garden a style appropriate for one rather specialized plant miss realizing the rich vitality and rewards that the many other plants can create in aggregate.

Ideal Versus Reality

When I started my search for a home, it really was a search for a plot of land where I could design and install a garden to my own specifications. I had a vision in mind of what my garden could ultimately be. Somehow, none of the places that I looked at came close to measuring up to this vision. In time, I came to realize that I would have to start with what was in order to build what could be. Certainly, there were some spectacular places with lush, fully mature gardens located in central Marin County. But such settings represented a fantasy that could not realistically be achieved with my limited budget resources.

In managing an organization, I have been continually challenged to bridge the gaps between my vision of the ideal, the reality of the present condition, and the resources actually available. Certainly, it is frustrating to have less time and money than one thinks is necessary to meet the standards and expectations of those involved. Too often, the budget is insufficient to hire all the staff, acquire all the new equipment, and provide all the support that seems to be ideal. I have found, however, that creatively working with the resources at hand is much more challenging and gratifying than buying instant results and success.

In the ideal world, one can conceive of and plant a garden from scratch, picking the ideal site as defined by its location, size, climate, terrain, soil conditions, sun exposure, and availability of resources such as water, fertilizer, and landscaping supplies. Living and working in California's Marin County, where scarcity of water means persistent rationing, I am ever mindful that critical resources for organizational success, just as with my garden, are often both expensive and in scarce supply. One must manage carefully in light of this reality.

Just as in the ideal world I might select a site with the optimum mix of perfect attributes, so also in my fantasy moods I speculate on what organization I might lead in such an ideal world. Depending on time and mood, this fantasy can take the form of speculations concerning client requests, suppliers, competitors, or employee relationships. Sometimes, in my dreams, we have an unlimited amount of computer equipment and incredibly powerful software. We are always highly motivated, energized, and working together harmoniously. At other times, we have the perfect office environment, with just the right amount of space available at the right time at the right price. And everything always works exactly as we want it to.

Reality quickly intrudes in the form of client expectations, employee relationships, and the myriad other considerations that are part of the responsibility of managing an organization. But when I review what our company has achieved, I readily conclude that it has been much more growth inducing and satisfying to deal with the real than the "ideal." In the real world, we start with what exists, confront the challenges as they come, and derive great satisfaction from doing so. This has also been my experience in gardening: it has been very gratifying to work within existing conditions. Rather than being limited by them, I have found that by developing a flexible plan and working conscientiously and with care, I have been able to create a garden that exceeds my original vision.

The Need for Rebuilding

When I inspected the property on which my new house was located, I found a garden that had once flourished but had fallen into disrepair with the owners' aging. This circumstance is certainly not unique to gardens. Organizations too can lose their compass and sense of direction, with disregard replacing regard, vibrancy and vitality turning into malaise and disinterest. Just as a garden is maintained in a beautiful state only by constant attention, so also is an organization.

The garden at my new home had been carefully planted and tended by a loving home gardener, a hobbyist rather than a professional. The layout was unsophisticated, with the location of plants being somewhat helter-skelter. It was like an organization where relationships of tasks and functions were not well thought out, or the physical locations of different units did not

58

relate functionally with others. The basic structure that is fundamental to a functioning garden had not been established. Privacy screens were missing, and the proximity of one type of plant to another was odd, if not incompatible with organic health. Most incongruous was the location of cactuses, which thrive in dry, sunny environments, planted next to and shaded by redwood trees, which thrive in moist coastal conditions. This choice and grouping of plants can be compared to organizations whose structure reflects an indifferent approach to the design and relationship of work units as well as to the selection of people for various positions. Sensitivity to the particular needs and personalities of the different departments and types of people performing certain tasks is not evident in such organizations.

Besides being both poorly maintained and made of disparate mixes of plants, the physical layout and organization of the garden were uninviting and nonfunctional. There were many straight, unidimensional concrete paths that sacrificed much of the pleasurable experience of transiting different parts of the garden. Much of the land area was highly underutilized, massive sloping slabs of concrete and heavy clay soil frustrating plant growth. The only plants that would grow in such undesirable soil conditions were weeds.

The dysfunctionality and infertility of the garden seemed to reflect conditions that I have seen imposed in organizations with rigid policies that smother innovation. Since both gardens and organizations are constantly evolving, their organizational design must accommodate change. Repressive organizational climates stifle all but the least imaginative individuals. Although some seem willing to accept such discouraging status quo conditions, I was emphatic that I would not have my vision of a beautiful garden impaired by these conditions. So I figured out what needed to be done, took on those tasks that I could do myself, and brought in help for tasks that were beyond my particular capabilities.

As enticed as I was by the idea that I would do all the work in the garden myself, I concluded that it would be wiser to hire someone to jackhammer up the excessive concrete than to take on that job myself. I did shovel out more truckloads of clay than I care to remember, taking them to another location where they effectively served as landfill. I replaced the clay with sand, manure, and such special supplements as rock phosphate, bone meal, ground seaweed, and various other locally available soil amendments. Converting what prevented the flourishing of my garden into landfill for another location has parallels in what I periodically observe in organizations: what doesn't make any sense in one setting sometime is quite appropriate in another. And by bringing to an organization that which is missing, one can create the potential for growth and progress.

Honoring Uniqueness

As I studied my garden in greater detail, I discovered that many plants had special features and characteristics that I had at first overlooked. I found that there were several unusual fruit trees whose distinctiveness I had not initially perceived. Further, on one of my walks through the garden, I encountered some potentially striking flowering shrubs that, because of poor pruning, had originally appeared as drab, sparse, and sickly. This experience in my garden taught me a lesson that I have relearned many times in interpersonal relationships in business: it is all too easy to overlook a person's potential, because a quick assessment cannot pick up the full depth and range of an individual. Just as plants bloom and flourish to different degrees in different circumstances, individuals can grow and change, given encouragement and opportunity.

In fact, until I had lived in my house for a whole year, I really did not have sufficient knowledge to make informed and responsible decisions about my garden. Until I had experienced all the seasons, observing the garden at different times of the year, on sunny and cloudy days alike, I did not fully understand what I was working with and the potential of my plants. Decisions that I might have made before I had this understanding would very likely have been misguided.

Just as making a decision on the basis of a casual, one-time review of a plant would have amounted to miscalculation, an individual's potential within an organization cannot be effectively measured in a cursory way. People who initially seem very impressive can turn out to be less than impressive over time. They are the organizational equivalent of annuals—flowers that look absolutely fantastic when they bloom but have no staying power. Other individuals, who on first blush appear unimpressive, can bloom and develop extraordinary staying power, growing in stature and substance over time. They stand tall and strong in their own right and support the growth of others, like a plant offering shade or serving as a wind screen.

Planning and Flexibility

Although I had some definite plans about what my garden could be when I first saw it, these plans have evolved over time. My plan is dynamic and fluid, rather than static and unchanging. This continual evolution of my planning, with the learning experience prompting me to revise my implementation plans, in many ways replicates my experience in a management role.

A recurring theme that I encounter in business strategy literature is the importance of planning as an ongoing process rather than a one-time, single event focused on *producing a plan*. Working in my garden has taught me this lesson in a way that the textbooks never could. Digging in the various areas of my garden, I discovered different types and depths of soil. Over time, as I gained more knowledge of the sun and shade patterns at different times of the day and through the different seasons, I revised my initial plans to reflect what I had learned. This experience in my garden has tracked my organizational experience: plans that do not get revised to reflect what has been learned become ever more inappropriate and ever more disconnected from their fundamental purpose.

Although I did not know it at the time, the process that I pursued in developing a plan to revitalize my garden to its full potential closely tracked the planning system that Alfred Chandler chronicles in his 1962 classic *Strategy and Structure: Chapters in the History of the Industrial Enterprise.* Chandler's planning model is common among corporations that achieve business success. It involves first establishing a business strategy, then designing an organizational structure consistent with that strategy, and finally making staffing decisions concerning individuals appropriate to work within that structure to implement the strategy.

When planning my garden, I started with an overall vision of what I wanted. From there, I formulated a strategy that reflected my personal values plus my assessment of the garden's condition and its potential, given the resources that might reasonably be expected to be available. Next, I assessed how the garden was organized, giving consideration to relationships of the physical space—the size and type of garden areas and how one area related to another—and determined how best to structure my garden to allow its beauty to be fully experienced. Finally, I addressed the specific "staffing" of my garden, considering what types of plants were appropriate for the structure and assessing how the existing plants met the profile.

Some plants that I expected to thrive did not. Others did so well that they crowded out their neighbors. When plants that thrived beyond expectations placed pressure on those that were falling far short of their potential, I had to make the difficult decision of whether to cut back the flourishing plant so as to protect the underperformer. This decision closely parallels decisions that managers often have to face. Such hard choices require balancing the needs and circumstances of the individual plants, which are often in conflict, as well as considering what will be best for the garden in aggregate.

Managers should make changes only with great care and deliberation. In managing my garden, I carefully considered whether modifying my desired structure to accommodate the existing plants would achieve results close to my ideals. I determined which misplaced plants were salvageable, which I could transplant, and which were either inappropriate or dying. Such decisions, involving people and plants alike, are very difficult and should be made only with compassion for the individual and responsibility for the overall organization.

Nurturing

My gardening experience has taught me that when I invite a plant into my garden, I assume responsibility for that plant, since I have made decisions crucial to the plant's prospective well-being. When I devote the appropriate caring and attention to my plants, they usually thrive. When I do not, they wither or even die.

When I bought my property, I was impatient to transform my garden from the poorly laid out and tended plot of land on which weeds prevailed where beautiful plants should bloom, to the flourishing garden that I envisioned. Soon, I realized that a lot of hard work was required. Of equal importance, I learned that if my efforts were not properly directed, the changes that I sought would be less than impressive and longer in coming.

Positive, meaningful, and lasting change would not occur instantaneously. Sure, I could get short-term gratification from planting annuals that would bloom brilliantly for a short period. But those plants that would have the biggest impact on establishing the character of my garden would take the longest time to mature. A tall tree is sometimes rather unattractive in its early years. In my managerial role, I have learned that results do not always occur instantaneously. As frustrating as it can be at times, I've had to learn to practice patience to achieve lasting growth and positive results.

Initially, I became frustrated with plants that did not do well, that failed to meet my expectations, that were slow growing or sparse rather than blooming and vital. Over time, however, I realized that there was a direct relationship between how much attention I devoted to the plant and how well the plant did. Applying this lesson to my work, I am clear that when a manager hires an individual to work in an organization, the manager controls many of the circumstances that will determine whether that individual can be successful. Equally important, that manager can influence many of the ongoing circumstances that will determine whether the individual can survive, let alone thrive, in the organization. Those managers who carefully select the right fit between the individual and the organization and then provide appropriate ongoing attention to the individual, are applying "lessons from the garden" to create a beautiful organization.

Changing the organization to accommodate the particular circumstances and interests of individuals can sometimes result in an outcome far better than was ever initially expected. Likewise, in my garden I have been continually surprised by extraordinary outcomes that were highly divergent from my original plans. Especially rewarding for me was observing the plants that I had placed in a particular part of the garden reseed themselves in the most unlikely locations, such as cracks in the retaining walls and out-of-the-way places that had previously been barren, providing vibrancy and color in most exciting and unexpected ways. So also has been my experience in organizations—some of the most extraordinarily wonderful things happen with the most surprising and unanticipated people.

Balance

One of the continual challenges in working in my garden is balancing my roles as a visionary leader, a manager overseeing the process, and the worker who implements what the leader visualizes and the manager directs. Necessarily, I fill all three roles with varying degrees of emphasis over time. I must admit that sometimes, especially after many hours in the hot sun pushing wheelbarrows of manure from one part of the garden to another, the worker part of me can lose sight of the vision. On other occasions, in my leader role, I grow frustrated that the manager part of me hasn't done a better job of organizing the garden to get the necessary work done at the level of quality and timing that I insist upon. Although it is nice to think that there is a clear delineation of work, my experience in my garden parallels much of my management experience: I have to simultaneously visualize, coordinate, and do. Balancing the managerial and "doing" tasks with visionary leadership is often a lot harder to achieve than it may seem. I know that my associates get frustrated at times that activity can lag too far behind the vision; on the other hand, the imperative for controls and information systems can obscure the vision of what our firm is really about and what is really important to us.

A New Business Paradigm

Many of those promoting the concept of the *new business paradigm* assert that business can be the catalyst for overall societal change. Indeed, futurist Willis Harman and others have suggested that business is the most viable and vibrant of society's institutions and that consequently, by default, business represents the best prospect for implementing major change. While many find this concept appealing on the surface, I believe the conclusion is inescapable that business itself must change dramatically before it can or should be expected to change society.

Business as a catalyst for societal change could be compared to the transplanting of a plant that has thrived in one garden under particular conditions and circumstances to a different garden where there are different conditions and circumstances. Sometimes the transplant works, sometimes it doesn't: either the "receiving" garden rejects the new arrival or, worse, the new arrival infects the whole garden with some kind of disease. I have learned to consider transplanting plants or implementing ideas that I have observed in other gardens with great care. I want to be very sure that the plant or idea that I am transplanting is right for my garden. Similarly, before business implements societal change, we should be very sure that these changes are ones that we really want.

If the business paradigm is to provide a model for societal change, I am more comfortable with the values of the agrarian age than many of those that have been practiced in the industrial era. In the agrarian age, there was a close connection among family, business enterprise, and the community. In many senses, the business unit and the family were inseparable; the community was comprised of groups of interdependent family-business units, bound together by common concerns, shared values, and the imperative of cooperation and mutual support. The family-business units in the agrarian age emphasized responsibility and collaborative teamwork. The economic work of the family-business units broadly involved a major component of nurturing in the raising of crops and animals. Although brute strength and daring were honored, so too was the ability to care for and protect animals and plants.

As articulated by strategic economist Stephen Roulac in *Renaissance of Place* (a work in progress), the nature of economic organization and the relationships between business units providing services for society are changing dramatically. By the time society had reached the industrial age, the fundamental values that characterized the agrarian age were less and less recognized. Concurrently, the institutions of family, business, and community were becoming separate, disconnected, and sometimes adversarial. Women largely assumed the responsibility for providing the linkage or connection among these three institutions.

With families and communities subjected to extraordinary pressures, closeness and commitment in relationships were sometimes subordinated to distance and distrust. It reminds me of the once flourishing but long neglected garden that I acquired many years ago. To reestablish my garden's vitality and to take it to a new level of beauty, much observation, planning, and hard work were necessary. Similarly, we should not think that significant positive change will come easily to society. As I learned in my garden, if one is prepared to observe, envision, plan, work, and nurture with patience, wonderful results can be achieved.

Values

As the long-held paternal orientation of business falls into disrepute, there is need for a reintegration of basic values. I have found that it is not enough for business to operate separately from and independently of the communities in which its stakeholders reside. Just as a garden is influenced by what happens on adjacent plots of land, so are our business and family institutions influenced by what happens in other families and businesses. I have learned that I cannot expect my associates to operate in isolation from their many important roles outside their role in our organization. I believe that a business that is insensitive to its associates' family roles is destined to fall far short of what it might achieve if it gave adequate attention to the consequences of its stakeholders' familial involvements and responsibilities.

This systems orientation and a wholistic approach in business organizations parallel lessons I have learned in my garden. I was motivated to create a garden to enjoy its beauty, to grow food for my table, to contribute to growth by nurturing individual plants, and to promote the sustenance of the garden in aggregate. I have found that an organization that is well tended and operating effectively manifests a distinctive and special beauty and provides sustenance to all involved. In my managerial role, I have derived great satisfaction from working with individuals to create and sustain a strong organization in aggregate.

Community

A well-tended organization, or garden, serves as an inspiration to the community. Not just those I invite to my home, but also neighbors and passers-by enjoy my garden. Likewise, when I come into contact with a particularly well-run organization, beyond the satisfaction derived from a positive encounter with excellence, I become inspired to aim even higher in my own endeavors.

Conclusion

Among the many lessons that I have learned and relearned in my gardening experience are the importance of engaging in planning as an ongoing process, rather than as a one-time event, and the incorporating of previous experience into the process. By viewing planning as a process, one can maintain flexibility and openness to unanticipated events. Effective management, whether of a garden or a business, also involves recognition of diversity and constant attention to individual needs. Patience is necessary to allow appropriate time to make considered, informed decisions. Care in making changes is key; every modification affects the overall system and the individuals whose care is entrusted to the gardener. The gardener's responsibility is significant in that every action and nonaction influences the health and success of those for whom she has responsibility. Combining visionary leadership with the implementation of managerial tasks is a delicate balancing act. The new business paradigm will be better served to the extent that lessons from our gardens are applied to our organizational gardening.

Part Two

Balance, Harmony, and Nurturing the Spirit

Balance: The Ultimate Challenge for the 21st Century
Marie Kerpan

Corporate Poverty: Lessons from Refugee Camps
Barbara Shipka

The Workplace as Spiritual Haven
Kim McMillen

Values for the Global Marketplace:
A Quest for Quality with a Difference
Jacqueline Haessly

Finding ways to maintain our balance, particularly in these times of accelerating change and global crisis, requires a special perspective. The authors in this part help us expand our vision and understanding by exploring ways to achieve balance between personal and professional values, harmonious relationships, and the nourishment of the human spirit in work.

Marie Kerpan suggests that the biggest challenge facing us as we approach the turn of the century is "the need to master the balancing act required for survival and growth as individuals, organizations, and societies within a global community." She proposes eight shifts from old to new paradigm thinking that will support our search for balance.

Another call for a more global way of thinking comes from Jacqueline Haessly, who encourages us to question the traditional ways of doing business and points to the "connectedness between government and corporate policies and their impact on people in our community and our world." Jacqueline discusses six global values that must be addressed not only by business but also by governmental, educational, religious, and social institutions.

Deep personal experience in Somali refugee camps provided the stimulus for Barbara Shipka to recognize what she calls "spiritual poverty" in business. Drawing a parallel similar to Kathleen Keating's gardening metaphor in Part One, she explains that she found "grief and terror" in both refugee camps and corporate offices, and cautions against the hazards of the relief process in both international work and corporate change.

Massive social change forces many people to seek a deeper dimension of themselves—to find some balance in their lives. Kim McMillen asks companies to consider providing personal and logistical support for employees undergoing spiritual transformation. The need to nurture employees in this way is very new to business, but once understood, it will help companies keep valuable employees by supporting them through times of personal crisis.

Marie Kerpan is vice-president at Drake Beam Morin, Inc., an international human resources management consulting firm and industry leader in corporate outplacement consulting. Her specialty is career development and transition consulting.

Originally from the East Coast, Kerpan started a management consulting practice in New York City following a ten-year career at Chase Manhattan Bank, where, as a vice-president, she performed a variety of line and staff functions in marketing and operations culminating in the management of the international private banking business in New York.

Kerpan is on the board of the Professional Women's Network in San Francisco. She is politically active and has produced seminars about political candidates and issues.

4

Balance: The Ultimate Challenge of the 21st Century

Marie L. Kerpan

The biggest challenge facing us as we approach the turn of the century is the need to master the balancing act required for survival and growth as individuals, organizations, and societies within a global community.

The rate of change has accelerated dramatically in our lifetime. On a personal level, we are struggling to keep up with the constant demands to anticipate and accommodate change. Time has become a precious and scarce commodity, and we find ourselves questioning the way we spend it. We worry about the quality of our lives. It's the rare individual who is able to balance work, play, solitude, and relationship to family, friends, and community. Most of us are just barely keeping our heads above water at work and/or with our immediate families.

In organizations, the challenge of operating profitably in an ever changing marketplace with increasingly unpredictable variables is intense. Add the need to provide a milieu that empowers employees while maintaining harmonious relationships with the larger community and the environment and we have a monumental task.

Balancing the needs and desires of the individual with the needs of the community—whether it be the family, the corporation, or society—is at the heart of the matter. One aspect of this balancing is the need to temper the race for wealth and power with the higher values of a civilized society, such as integrity, prudence, compassion, and authenticity. Another aspect is the need for women to assume a larger role in leadership and management in order to provide a more balanced perspective.

Balance requires that standards be set and adhered to. We have become a nation with very low personal and professional standards. Standards have to do with how individuals go about their daily lives—managing themselves, relating to others and to their environment. The following are some thoughts about paradigm shifts in support of the drive toward balance and corporate and societal health.

Old Paradigm #1: *The corporate mission is to increase shareholder wealth.*

New Paradigm: *The corporate mission is to produce a quality service or product that promotes the well-being of the community and to provide a working environment conducive to personal growth and creative productivity while increasing shareholder wealth.*

It's not a bad idea (in the abstract) for corporations to strive to increase shareholder wealth. Untempered by parameters of responsibility, however, this goal can lead to a Machiavellian mentality.

The old paradigm has taken its toll in terms of the exploitation of natural and human resources to produce an abundance of redundant products and services, many of questionable value and quality. Of course, it has also produced ingenious, life-enhancing products and services, but the question of whether a product or service adds value is not considered important compared with its profitability.

The recently recognized need for conservation requires that we more carefully consider the value of what we produce. The United States has been recklessly exploiting natural resources as though the supply were infinite and we were the only people on the planet. The day of reckoning when we will be held accountable by our global neighbors for our waste and greed is surely coming. We need to revisit the notion that increasing wealth at any cost is a god-given right. There is a need to balance the variables of production and consumption so that the whole community is best served.

There are unlimited ways to improve the quality of life and make money doing so. If we apply our creativity and industriousness to figuring out how to make the world work for everyone, the idea of spending time, energy, and resources producing yet another sugary breakfast cereal will seem ridiculous (if it doesn't already).

Our supermarkets reflect both our extraordinary riches and the lunacy of our mindless production and consumption with their shelf-loads of chemical-laden, nutritionally anemic foodstuffs. People are starving in our own country, not to mention the rest of the world, while we have at least fifty types of cookies in every supermarket, to name only one embarrassing example. Furthermore, it's quite possible, if not likely, to fill your shopping cart and end up with a nutritionally deficient diet.

If we went through the supermarket and removed all of the items that are not components of a healthy diet, we would be amazed at how little was left. The mind boggles to think about how many people spend their lives producing this stuff. Why would anyone consciously spend their life producing a product that is not healthy for human beings? To increase shareholder wealth?

What about the working environment? In the new paradigm workplace, people are treated as the most valuable asset, and their concerns and well-being are given top priority. This is a radical departure from the status quo, despite the amount of lip service given to such ideas. Child care, parental leave, flextime, first-class facilities, and equitable compensation would be the natural concerns of corporations. Employees' creativity would be encouraged and rewarded, and their personal growth would be cultivated.

In those rare corporations where such practices already exist, the payoff in productivity, product and service quality, and profits has been documented. Unfortunately, the message is slow to enter the mainstream.

The third dimension in the new paradigm corporate mission is the impact of the production process on the community and the environment. The new corporation must take seriously its responsibility to the community—economically, socially, and ecologically. The idea of big business lobbying to relax or eliminate federal standards designed to prevent pollution and preserve natural resources (because such standards interfere with the ability to generate profits) just doesn't make sense from the perspective of the new paradigm. It's not a balanced perspective.

The rationale that jobs will be lost if these standards are enforced is shortsighted (another hallmark of the status quo). The kinds of changes that we need to undertake to restore balance in our work lives and society will require enormous dislocation. The upside is the wealth of new opportunities that will emerge—a veritable new frontier. Unfortunately, the way to the new frontier is through uncharted territory, and the passage will be uncomfortable.

Old Paradigm #2: *Every man for himself.*

New Paradigm: *Managing one's personal and material growth in the context of the larger community.*

Every man for himself is a micro version of Old Paradigm #1. It is a myopic perspective applied at the personal level. It reflects the importance of the individual (or the few) over the good of the community.

Our culture exalts individual freedom. This pivotal value is woven throughout the fabric of our society. This value requires modification to be in sync with a context shift toward balance. When we try to balance the needs of the individual with the needs of the community, we tread on very sacred ground.

Yet much of our present suffering is directly related to our isolation and alienation from the community. Greed, crime, substance abuse, power abuse, and sloth are, at least in part, a response to isolation and alienation. Furthermore, we are cracking under the strain of trying to do everything ourselves. It's easier to share the load. More can be accomplished in less time by a group effort. The problems we're facing can be solved only by pulling together—in a community effort.

In corporate life, the old paradigm often produces managers and leaders who are more concerned with self-aggrandizement (personal accumulation of wealth and power) than they are with carrying out their duties responsibly. We see this phenomenon in the skyrocketing compensation of senior executives of failed and failing corporations.

In the public sector, our government is gridlocked by trying to accommodate an endless array of demands from different constituencies all staking their claims to individual freedoms—to bear arms, to sell pornography, to burn flags, to be gay, to raze virgin forests, to have abortion on demand, and so forth. As if this weren't complicated enough to negotiate, many of our government representatives are primarily concerned with how to retain their positions. Under these conditions, is it any wonder that we seem to be impotent in the face of our cultural and economic decline?

We are missing an appropriate framework for decision making and conflict resolution based on what's best for the whole community.

Old Paradigm #3: *Leadership by white males.*

New Paradigm: *Representative leadership including women and minorities.*

The most glaring imbalance in the leadership status quo is the absence of women. Would things be different if women were equally represented? We do have some experience in the workplace—ironically, less in government than in private industry. Many of us have witnessed significant shifts in corporate cultures where women have advanced. The corporate conversation is altered by the presence of women (tokenism excepted).

Priorities change, different values come into play, a different point of view is expressed. Because women have been outsiders for so long, one of the real benefits that they bring to the party is a healthy disrespect for the status quo—for the traditional way of doing and looking at things. This new perspective may initiate, and in some cases is initiating the revitalization and transformation that are so badly needed.

Paternalistic management style is being replaced by a more consensus-driven management style, often described as a more feminine style. Managers can no longer afford to keep their people in the dark about what's really going on in exchange for "protection." The challenges of today's business environment require full participation and teamwork. Employees are no longer willing to be treated like children.

It seems axiomatic that representative leadership (including appropriate representation by gender, race, and ethnicity) would bring a more dynamic approach to problem solving and be more likely to create a work environment better suited to the well-being of the community. Furthermore, if employees felt more affinity with their leaders, morale and loyalty might improve.

Old Paradigm #4: *Conforming to the status quo as a value.*

New Paradigm: *Embracing diversity and encouraging self-expression in the context of group responsibility.*

One of the striking characteristics of our workplace and culture is boredom and stagnation. It is paradoxical that our culture exhorts "doing your own thing" but at the same time rewards and extols a narrow band of "acceptable" behaviors. As a consequence, instead of feeling free to do or be anything, we feel constricted by socially and politically "correct" choices. It's ironic that we have the means and the freedom to do much more than almost any other society, yet our value system has the power to eviscerate our creativity.

Our culture idolizes the business world for its potential to generate unlimited wealth. In comparison to Europe, for example, we place a disproportionate value on being a business professional. In our society, only sports and entertainment have the same cachet. The reason is that we most value the professions wherein you can make the most money, period. Teachers, artists, writers, and other professionals enjoy higher status in Europe than in the United States. Life-style (especially in terms of leisure time) has a much higher priority in Europe than the accumulation of wealth and power. In our country, if you aren't flat out "going for it" at all times, you are considered an underachiever.

One of the crises going on in the workplace, especially among "baby boomers," is the disenchantment with corporate America. There's widespread boredom, disgust, and burnout with corporate life, but the work force is trapped by "golden handcuffs" and life-styles that depend on high incomes. Walking the halls of the outplacement firms, one sees evidence that American industry is outplacing its best and brightest because they're boat rockers and don't conform to the corporate status quo.

The cultural imperative in many of our corporations is for each employee to manage perception, protect his or her own interests, promote him- or herself, and compete with colleagues with the ultimate goal of acquisition of wealth and power. There is often little appreciation of creativity, collaboration, critical thinking, planning, and holistic management.

In the old paradigm, managers tend to set up hierarchies that are fairly autocratic and espouse a relatively inflexible set of norms. For example, there is a tendency to follow the leader in dress, speech, mannerism, and especially ideology. The ambitious must attend carefully to the set of prescribed behaviors that win acceptance. The mavericks (and people who are the "wrong" race or gender) aren't likely to advance. The stultifying effect of such a closed system is incompatible with the needs of the modern corporation. The need to respond to the constantly changing environment demands eclectic and creative thinking. We need to encourage the expression of diversity instead of trying to suppress it. We don't have our eye on the ball, and it shows in our inability to sustain our position of leadership in the world.

The human cost of this conformist orientation is significant—boredom, indifference, cynicism, and inauthenticity. Some of us no longer believe that we make a difference because the cards are stacked against us. Disappointed and disempowered by our leaders for too long, we've abdicated responsibility. Consequently, the system perpetuates itself and casts off the challengers. We see this in government as well as private industry.

There is a deadening homogeneity pervading our workplace from coast to coast, stifling our ability to motivate ourselves and others to achieve, produce, and create. Our wealth and freedom, which can produce miracles, have fallen far short of our expectations for self-actualization, satisfaction, and quality of life.

Old Paradigm #5: *Blaming big business and government for our personal and societal problems.*

New Paradigm: *Taking responsibility for our own lives and our communities, both at home and at work.*

This is a principle very much at the heart of transformational thinking. People are waking up to the fact that they are responsible for the quality of their own lives. Blaming mom and dad for the way we turned out just doesn't cut it anymore. Similarly, blaming the boss, the corporation, or the government is pointless and only reinforces the "us versus them" mentality. We are at the stage of the game where if we're not part of the solution, we're part of the problem.

Thankfully, there are signs of awakening to this reality everywhere. After years of complaining about the government and the politicians, people are starting to take matters into their own hands and participate in our democracy by paying more attention to who is running for office. Many people have answered the call to political activism and are surprised and delighted to find their actions making a difference. More than one congressional representative has been replaced by a dark-horse candidate, often a woman.

In the corporate arena, the rank and file are growing intolerant of incompetent and irresponsible management. The recent focus on executive compensation is the tip of the iceberg. As the baby boomers transit the midlife passage, they're asking a lot of questions of themselves and of their leaders. "Why are we doing this?"—shades of the '60s.

People going through midlife typically reexamine their values. Because the bulk of the population is currently dealing with this phase of life, we may be approaching the critical mass required for a needed paradigm shift.

Another example of the trend toward self-actualization is the growing tendency of people to change careers. Again, the baby boomers are leading the fray, many of them as a result of layoffs. They're examining their work lives and assessing how well suited they are to their work and how much satisfaction they're getting from their careers.

This examination often reveals that they did not choose their careers rationally. They fell into them by chance and stayed for twenty years only to discover that they don't really enjoy what they have been doing and perhaps are ill suited to it. Taking responsibility for one's satisfaction at work is one of the biggest challenges in life and one for which we are woefully unprepared by our parents, our educational system, and our culture. Meeting this challenge requires courage and persistence but the rewards are incalculable for the individual, the workplace, and the community.

Old Paradigm #6: *Acceptance of duplicity as a way of being.*

New Paradigm: *Authenticity as a standard in all human affairs.*

Duplicity takes two main forms in our culture:

- It's acceptable to say or do anything to accomplish your goal provided you are not caught in the act. Lying and other forms of dishonesty, while not approved of, are definitely tolerated and generally not punished in business and government.

- It's acceptable to maintain a public and private persona that are not subject to the same standards.

It's hard even to imagine what life would be like if people were authentic—if they said what they meant all the time and you could count on their word. Was there ever a time like that? Was it ever better than it is now? Or, in the "old days," was there just a tighter lid on accurate information?

For all the criticism leveled at the media for invasion of privacy and muckraking, a great deal of truth has been revealed by our free press. The sad truth is that our leaders lie to us routinely, and without an active and free press, we would have a very different view of what is going on. The control of information is a trump card in politics, government, and business. We do know, however, that our leaders tell us what they want us to hear and that this may have nothing whatever to do with the truth—a sobering thought.

Do we have the wherewithal to change this? Let's hope so. Given today's era of instant information, it's increasingly difficult for people in leadership positions to conceal duplicitous behavior.

Television has given us access to firsthand multisensory information. As we watch the U.S. Congress in session, we gain insight into our political and legislative process that was simply not available before. The impact is profound on many levels, even though the images and data that are presented are still edited and shaped by the media (and others). Consider the impact of the Clarence Thomas hearings. We were able to judge for ourselves who was telling the truth, taking into account our intuitive responses about the authenticity of each individual. This event was a "galvanizer"—mobilizing many women to become politically active.

Our headlines are filled with daily stories of scandal. In government, private industry, and nonprofit and religious institutions, the stories of duplicitous behavior on the part of our leaders are rampant, whether it be lying, cheating, stealing, sexual indiscretion, or abuse. How is it that so many scoundrels manage to work their way into high places? Could it be that these people represent the norm? Is duplicitous behavior normative in our society? High-profile people are subject to closer scrutiny and are caught in the act more often than the guy next door. Leaders usually play for higher stakes than the average citizen, so transgressions often seem outrageous. But maybe it's only a question of degree.

We no longer expect the truth from our leaders and managers. We take what they say with a grain of salt. It's hard to imagine how we expect to make headway in solving the monumental problems we're facing if we can't believe or trust each other and our leaders. This area desperately needs a paradigm shift.

On the bright side, there are those individuals who aspire to authenticity and work hard to live up to that standard. Doing so in the existing paradigm can seem like a no-win proposition, but it's not necessarily so. Living authentically is its own reward, and we would do well to choose our leaders by this standard.

Old Paradigm #7: *Competing in the context of a win-lose model.*

New Paradigm: *Collaborating in the context of a win-win model.*

This is the toughest paradigm to shift, because it's inbred in men. From the little league to the military and all the stops in between, men are taught to compete for everything. This is in sharp contrast with women, who are taught to cooperate and share rather than compete.

The '80s have taken their toll on our population. It was a win-lose decade. The top 1 percent of the population won, and the rest lost ground. We're experiencing an unprecedented polarization between the haves and the have-nots. The concentration of wealth and power in the hands of a few is the definition of an oligarchy, a win-lose model.

As women advance in business and government, we're seeing a shift toward cooperation and collaboration. This shift is imperative for peaceful coexistence within communities. Corporations are a perfect microcosm in which to test win-win strategies for worker, customer, and shareholder satisfaction, and the corporation's relationship to the environment and the community. These institutions have the resources and the expertise to manage change. Unfortunately, corporations also have the biggest stake in preserving the status quo.

On the bright side, with the end of the cold war, we're seeing an unprecedented move toward global collaboration. Governments are working together in the interest of world peace. It would be nice to see more collaboration between our government and private industry in addressing domestic issues here at home.

Old Paradigm #8: *Valuing form over substance.*

New Paradigm: *Valuing substance over form.*

"Looking good" is critically important in the existing paradigm. Hence the importance of image in the political and business arenas. Unfortunately, looking good may have nothing to do with being competent, qualified, or even understanding, much less caring about the responsibilities of one's office.

Managing perception is the name of the game, and it is discussed quite openly in the workplace. Information is routinely distorted, if not fabricated, to produce the desired impression. "Perception is the reality" is the lesson taught by corporate America. While this may be quite true philosophically, it is a message that, when misconstrued, results in delusional thinking.

We even have an entire industry devoted to creating and managing image. It's called advertising. We're primed to want the right stuff in order to gain status. Dress for success. Drive a sexy car. Wear the right labels. We have become adept at acquiring the symbols of success (often going into debt to do it). We actually operate as though it were more important to *look* good than to *be* good. It's a kind of magical thinking. Why go to the trouble of working hard and becoming accomplished when all you really need is to "get your act together"?

This image consciousness is reflected in the way senior managers are selected. The packaging is of tantamount importance—the right schools, the right social and business contacts, the right clothes, the right demeanor, the right sex, the right color. It's also important that they be willing to play the game as loyal team members—no boat rocking. It's astonishing how little substantive information changes hands during the interviewing process for most management positions. Decisions are made based on the basis of "chemistry" and packaging.

It's common for a highly qualified and competent candidate to be passed over because he or she doesn't fit the mold. Not only does this practice jeopardize the health of an organization, it sends a debilitating message to the troops about the likelihood of any meaningful change and the possibility of making a difference. The game is rigged!

Valuing form over substance has lethal consequences. It produces the phenomenon of the "empty suit" (leaders who, by rational and intelligent criteria, would not be selected for positions of authority). It produces leaders whose qualifications are primarily how they look, whom they know, and how wealthy they are. They're unqualified by experience, knowledge, wisdom, integrity, intelligence, or maturity. This phenomenon is epidemic in both the public and private sectors. Where is our appreciation of intelligence, good judgment, prudence, critical thinking, and maturity? Why aren't we basing choices and decisions on these substantive qualities?

Conclusion

When we consider how far we have to go to achieve balance, it's easy to get discouraged. But unless we come to grips with what's not working, we can't begin the creative dialogue about how to fix it. The bad news is that we as a country have not owned up to the truth about what's not working. There is a lot of denial at all levels of our society about what is really going on—dysfunctional families produce dysfunctional societies. The good news is that every day there is movement in the right direction. The paradigms are shifting. It's up to each of us to do our part to reveal the truth and take action in the faith that what we do makes a difference.

Barbara Shipka provides consulting focused on assisting individuals and groups to more fully develop their potential so that they may both enjoy and succeed at surfing on the waves of change. Her approach is to work primarily within the context of ongoing organizational processes, fostering and facilitating creativity, innovation, and experimentation and furthering the organization's vision. Among her corporate clients are Cray Research, Alliant Techsystems, Honeywell, IDS Financial Services, Medtronic, The Pillsbury Company, and Wilson Learning.

During her career, Shipka has also worked in the government and nonprofit sectors, including the United Nations and the field of education. She has lived and worked in Lebanon, the Dominican Republic, Somalia, Ethiopia, The Sudan, Czechoslovakia, and Switzerland, and she has spent time in many other parts of the world.

5

Corporate Poverty: Lessons from Refugee Camps

Barbara Shipka

For three years during the mid-1980s, I took a hiatus from my corporate consulting practice to work in Somalia, The Sudan, and Ethiopia under the auspices of the U.N. High Commission for Refugees and the governments of those countries. The work was financially supported by the U.S. government and delivered through nongovernmental organizations. In each of the projects, my work focused on assisting others in developing managerial skills and increasing creativity and collaboration among all the agencies and programs working with refugees.

Dateline Somalia

Though it was early morning, the day was already hot. The sun was shining in the way that bleaches everything. Everything, that is, except for the colors created by the dresses and head wraps of women who gathered to draw water from the well. As far as I could see, there were igloo-shaped huts, thousands upon thousands of them made from materials of the desert and from the plastic and burlap in which food had arrived.

The camp commander invited me into the hut that served as his office and asked me to be seated. My Somali co-workers and the elders who followed me in squatted. As my eyes adjusted to the darkness, I began to look around. There were about fifteen of us, and one bench, upon which I sat. The floor was hardened earth. As I assessed my surroundings, I began to realize that the bench had been brought in from somewhere especially for me. I was aware that these people were managing a refugee camp with a fluctuating population that was currently in the range of 40,000 people. And yet here I was in the camp commander's office—no desks, no paper, no filing cabinets, no telephones, no secretaries, no pens or pencils, no procedure manuals, no clocks, no anything!

Now, more than ever, I wondered what I was doing here. I felt humbled to the very marrow of my bones. How presumptuous of me! What could I possibly bring to this party? I did not speak either Oromo or Somali. I did not understand the cultures, let alone the clash of cultures! What I understood about management and organization consulting, and what I considered useful at home, clearly was not going to be particularly useful in this situation.

In addition to the fear and anxiety I had experienced during my first weeks in Somalia, and the sense of isolation I felt without my network, my reputation, my books, and familiar surroundings to lean on, I was now in the pit of despair. It all seemed so huge and overwhelming and hopeless. Why bother?

As I look back, I know I made a useful contribution. But more importantly, my time in Africa made a priceless, immeasurable contribution to me. My personal experience of having nothing to draw on except what's inside me and my opportunity to witness others drawing on themselves in the same way reinforced my sense that wisdom and other needed resources are within each of us, waiting to be called out. This inner wisdom can lead us through apparently impossible circumstances. The learnings I gained through working in the famine- and war-stricken regions of Africa have become the basis for much of my work in corporations.

Striking Similarities

Having become vividly aware of the obvious differences between corporate businesses and refugee camps, I was amazed to recognize striking similarities between them. My experiences in the world of international relief and development have become a useful analogy for me to see that I am still working with poverty, and I am still encouraging myself and others to draw out and rely on the deep wisdom inside ourselves.

In refugee camps, physical poverty is at its starkest. Most of us have seen the pictures on TV—the ones that are so difficult to watch—of dying children with distended bellies, toothpick limbs, and pleading eyes. People arrive in the camps with nothing and are completely dependent on others for their very lives. That is why they come. It is their one known means of staying alive. It is poverty on the physical level.

In many corporations, poverty also exists. It is "spiritual poverty" at its starkest. For large numbers of people, the workplace occupies a majority of their waking hours, and for many, it is the most important place in their lives. It is where they seek meaning and purpose.

We in the corporate setting tend to believe that we are supposed to check our deepest personal selves—our inner lives, our soul's development—at the door of the workplace, at least publicly. This assumption prevents us from bringing some of the most powerful and creative parts of ourselves to our jobs. In corporations, fear, anxiety, a sense of isolation, apathy, and despair are the results of spiritual poverty, and their effects on us are similar to the disease, starvation, and death in refugee camps.

These are scary thoughts, I know. Yet in each of the images that follow, the elements of anxiety, isolation, and despair are highlighted to differing degrees. If you work in a corporation, you have lived similar experiences.

- I spoke with a client who had been promoted to a high-level executive team with members from all over the world. She said, "I know we need to get to know each other in order to be most productive, but we just don't have time. In fact, when someone stops me in the hall to speak with me, I find myself thinking, 'Could you just get on with it? I'm too busy for this.'" She has relegated one of the primary functions of human existence—connecting with people—to being just one more task in an already too task-filled life.

- As I was interviewing a person about her work situation, I heard her rage and despair. I asked her whether she felt that there was any hope at all for improving her work environment and the relationships in it. "No," she sobbed, "I really don't think there is any hope at all. And I feel so helpless." These thoughts and feelings were echoed by most of the people I interviewed in her group.

- A middle manager who had enormous interpersonal problems with the people he managed was mostly oblivious to those problems. But he was very concerned about how the people above him in the hierarchy saw him. He said to me, "I need to polish my image with upper management. I need to learn how to present myself better. That's how people get ahead in this company. It's not by being real."

- I was working with three upper-level managers who had taken on responsibility for launching a high-visibility venture within a large corporation. They were experiencing extreme pressure from executive management, they felt highly visible, and didn't believe that they had the resources required to do their best. As I worked with these three, I saw them becoming scared, angry, and depressed. I actually saw the grayness—the draining out of vitality—in each of their faces.

It is easy for us to see the impact of physical poverty if we choose to look. It ravages the faces and bodies of people who experience it. Spiritual poverty is not necessarily as easy to see or to recognize. We live with it daily in our corporations and we become numb to it. What we do see and feel we don't talk about.

When we realize what we are missing, feelings deeper than fear and anxiety—feelings of grief and terror—come to the surface. "What have I missed by not noticing my feelings at work all these years?" and "What if I can't get back in touch?" or "What if I take a risk and get punished?"

The Need to Feel

I was working with a company president who reacted negatively and quite forcefully to my suggestions about how he might be able to connect more fully with other people in his company. As I reflected, I realized that for him to decide to make major changes in his perspective, let alone his style, would mean opening up and reviewing decades of decisions that he had made on the basis of his current set of assumptions. It was a potential Pandora's box.

If we can get through the feelings of grief and terror, despair surfaces next. "Why bother trying? It's all so hopeless. The amount of isolation that I feel and see around me is enormous. And the need to always look competent is so entrenched in the system that we'll never be able to make it any different."

I recently visited a company that has done much to address issues of spiritual poverty. There are no memos. There is a community meeting in the mornings. People spend time enlisting each other's support even across functions. Parents are provided with cribs by their work stations and are encouraged to bring new babies to work with them. They have an on-site day-care center. Food in the cafeteria is hearty and healthy.

I suggested that since they have done so much for themselves, it was time for them to share the "how to's" with other corporations. One person said, "I've tried many times. And I get responses like, 'Easy for you to say, you're in a young company,' and 'Maybe you can afford to, but we can't.' And I tell them that they can't afford *not* to."

Despair is the last step to the bottom of the pit. If we can push through the despair, we can get out of the pit. We can begin to draw on our wisdom—the wisdom that can lead us through apparently impossible circumstances. When we draw from our core, we realize that we are essentially safe; that security comes from within rather than from another person or a job. We can tell the truth to ourselves and to each other, we can be open about who we are, bring new and different ideas to the table, take risks and get rewarded or at least supported, express our feelings and points of view and be fully heard, make our individual needs known. We can create safe spaces for each other, cherish the differences that inevitably arise, and use conflict as a creative force. We can take responsibility for ourselves and respect each other. This is the arena of relationship. This is the arena of creativity and innovation. This is the arena that values the human spirit. This is the arena of authenticity.

Authenticity

Much is being said these days about the power of relationship in the workplace. The phrases used are "building teams," "partnerships," and "alliances," both within and beyond the boundaries of organizations. The belief is that this power of relationship is an untapped resource for businesses, a resource that can provide a competitive edge. This is true. But it is not relationship itself that is the core possibility. Relationship is the result. It is the result of *authenticity*. And authenticity is the result of tapping the spiritual well, the wisdom within. Therefore, the actual competitive edge is in consciously addressing conditions that result in spiritual poverty within each individual.

So what do we do? We actually are already doing a lot— from quality circles to employee involvement, from valuing diversity to building community, from participation to empowerment. Call them what you will, all of these initiatives request and require people to bring more of themselves to work—to draw more from within, to be more authentic. By embarking on these initiatives, we provide the means of countering spiritual poverty within the business context.

A Model

The model of relief and development in the world at large provides a road map for spiritual relief and development in organizations. There are several aspects to the process of providing relief, whether physical or spiritual. First, we must acknowledge the emergency—no matter how painful—and provide relief in order to minimize further damage. We also must recognize hazards of the relief process.

Relief treats symptoms but not systemic causes. It creates dependency and counterdependency and establishes expectations that cannot be met over time. There is always the aftermath experience of the emergency to be tended.

Relief is a critical and essential step in a process, but it is insufficient and incomplete in and of itself. In order to overcome the hazards, more complete development processes are required. Relief is preparation for a more complete process of development. Let me elaborate.

1. Acknowledge the Emergency and Provide Relief

The drive across the Sudanese desert to the area of the refugee camps had taken all day. I had seen carcass after carcass of cows and camels and goats lying dead along the road, having dropped in their tracks. The government official told me that satellite photos were being taken of the movements of people. He said, "Hundreds of thousands of them are walking in our direction. We have to be as ready as we can to receive them. Hundreds of people are arriving every day. All of our food and water must be trucked in, the desert nights are cold and we don't have enough blankets, doctors and nurses are working around the clock..."

I heard the words, but it wasn't until later that night, when I was in the nearby town, that I understood. Everywhere there were people walking. It was as though something special was

95

soon to occur. But I knew different. I knew that this walking meant that people had lost their homes, that they were hungry, that many were ill and some were dying. Returning to the camp, I understood even better. I saw people waiting everywhere, hoping to get in through the gate when it opened in the morning.

Given these circumstances, the principle of triage underlies the actions of people. Triage can be characterized as "Save as many lives as you can. Some people will die. So be it. Locate and treat the ones you think have the best chance of staying alive. Just do what you have to do to get the job done. We'll regroup when this emergency is over."

This description of an emergency in Africa is analogous to what occurs in corporate settings when people are viewed as a commodity. In "Evolution and Business" from his forthcoming book *The Universal Human*, Gary Zukav points out that when we view employees as a "resource," they can be used in much the same way that electricity or raw materials are used. The consequences of viewing people as a commodity are especially vivid under conditions such as new start-up businesses, downsizing, and major shifts in strategy due to market pressures.

During an emergency stage in corporate organizations, all parts of the system experience tremendous stress. The experience of triage results in people working harder, for longer hours, with fewer resources available and more perfection expected than ever before. People are aware that their very jobs and livelihood are at stake. Groups have goals that stretch them beyond what seems like reality. Businesses are fighting for profitability, fighting to stay in business.

One group that I work with has handled their new business start-up with some humor. It is humorous but not funny. They struggle daily against their work for balance in their total lives. In jest, one employee was overheard to say, "Look, if you can't come in on Saturday, just don't bother to come in on Sunday at all." And on one Saturday morning, the receptionist was actually heard saying, "No, I'm sorry. He's not in. He's on vacation this weekend."

But another group had some bitterness. Their organization had laid off several thousand people at the same time that the hole was being excavated for the foundation of a large new corporate headquarters. One of the "jokes" making the rounds was that the hole was actually a mass grave for all those being laid off.

The consequences of the stresses of "corporate emergency" can be tragic. One woman spoke of taking her laundry to her mother's house because she was working fifteen- and sixteen-hour days and just couldn't get it done. On her way home, she was in a car accident. She said that, with the stress of her job, the lack of time for the rest of her life, and how lonely she felt, her dream job had turned into a nightmare.

The beliefs, norms, and expectations of organizations have caused many people to deprive themselves of spiritual food. In reality, feeding ourselves spiritually at work is essential to our survival. The consequences of becoming spiritually impoverished are overwhelming. Fear, anxiety, isolation, apathy, and despair claim significant amounts of creative energy. When these conditions exist, people are often afraid of being exposed as inadequate—and they are. They are malnourished as a result of spiritual poverty.

2. Hazards of the Relief Process

• *Relief Treats Symptoms but Not Systemic Causes*

I stood to the side and watched as people waited to collect their weekly rations of rice, oil, and powdered milk. The relief workers and refugees who worked with them were shouting to each other, making sure that every station was covered, knowing that once they began the routine morning distribution process, there'd be no stopping until everyone who was to receive food got what they had come for. In contrast to conditions months earlier, these people now had a source of food and water, they had shelter, and they had some medical support. In most of them, I witnessed a significant improvement in their health—a return of life force, but not necessarily well-being or vitality. Their basic needs were being met but the future was unknown for them.

97

Relief is temporary. It does not have staying power. I found my work in Africa full of meaning. I also was aware that providing the direct services of relief was changing nothing about the big picture. We were saving people's lives—but only as long as the food continued to arrive.

To draw a corporate comparison, I was called in on an emergency basis to work with a group where there was a lot of conflict and people wanted their manager fired. Everyone's patience was extremely short, all the way up to the vice-president. He entertained the possibility of cutting the entire group out of the organization and purchasing the services from outside contractors. Through a team building intervention, we were able to restore enough hope to the group that they could proceed with their work. But the intervention was entirely for the purpose of *relief*—not development. The relief served only as a prelude to further development. As we got beneath the interpersonal conflicts, the issues that surfaced were not personal but were organizational in nature. They had to do with how work was organized, with duplications and gaps, how employees in this group were being measured differently from those in other groups, and how the larger organization unknowingly thwarted them as they attempted to get their jobs done. All of these issues were long-term development opportunities.

Beneath the symptoms of relationship issues that relief addresses, there will always be development opportunities. If the immediate symptoms can be treated and relieved and the context can be enlarged enough to identify underlying causes, a group that may have thought its life was over can achieve excellence in the long term.

• Relief Creates Dependency and Counterdependency

I arrived in Beirut, Lebanon, in the summer of 1970, right during the height of the hijackings by Palestinian terrorists. At the time, I just couldn't comprehend what would prompt people my age to sacrifice their lives and the lives of others by blowing up airplanes. A Palestinian friend told me, "Please understand, people who are twenty years old now have spent their entire lives in these camps. They have no sense of a better future for themselves. They hear their parents speak of the lives they once had. These stories tell of lives that were modest—a home, a donkey, some goats, perhaps an orchard. Nothing more. But that was enough to provide meaning and dignity to their lives."

Relief creates dependency. People in poverty become dependent on others for their existence. There is a point—when death is the alternative—at which this dependency is important. It supports people through the weakness that resulted from the poverty. It allows people to glimpse light through their hopelessness and despair. But if the dependency looks as though it will be permanent, the hopelessness and despair return—now accompanied by low self-respect, loss of meaning, and anger at the source of the relief.

I had a very painful experience with this hazard. While working in a very exciting, fast-paced, innovative organization, I was asked to assist cross-functional teams in becoming more effective. People in the organization were pleased with the results. I became more and more involved with the organization. I recognized the hazard of dependency and periodically attempted to disengage. I was told, "You can't just fire yourself. It's important that you not leave us now. There's still a lot for you to do. We'll know when the time is right." I stayed on. And I stayed on. And then, when I had become heavily engaged in the culture of the organization, something began to change—slowly at first, and then more and more. A few people became angry. I was left out of situations in which I had been included before. They were trying to disengage me, and now I didn't want to go. I remember the lonely pit in my stomach. What had initially been dependency on their part had became counterdependency. I was now dependent on them as well.

The dependency and counterdependency issues in organizations are enormous. We have so much learning to do about what's helpful, what's not; about when dependency is useful, when it's not; about empowerment, control, responsibility, accountability. Therefore, it's important to distinguish the initial dependency of relief that *allows* the possibility of further development to take place from the dependencies that rob people of their opportunities to be empowered and self-sufficient.

- *Relief Establishes Expectations That Cannot Be Maintained over Time*

On a visit to Asmara, I spent a morning with a monk of the Ethiopian Catholic Church who was managing food distribution in the region. In his office was a blackboard, and on the blackboard was a grid. Across the top were the months of the year, and down the side were the names of villages in the region. In the boxes were numbers. I asked him to explain it to me. He said that it reflected the amount of food that was being distributed. It was now February. I noticed that beginning with April and onward, several of the boxes that previously had held numbers such as 10,000, and 20,000, and 40,000 now had X's through them. Again I asked him to explain. He told me that beginning in April, the Poles would be taking back the helicopters that they had lent to the effort. They had other needs for the helicopters. And the villages with X's through them were villages that were basically inaccessible except by air because of the war that was going on.

I was appalled and deeply saddened. "What will happen?" I asked. "Those people have no more food and no more ability to get food than they did before. Isn't that true?"

"Yes," he responded as he sighed. "The world's attention has shifted to other matters such that people think the drought and famine have passed."

This story corresponds to what happens in organizations when resources become scarce. Efforts that provide spiritual food, such as skills training that can help people to be more effective and tools that assist people to be more efficient, are often cut back or cut out altogether. "Headcounts" is reduced, and jobs that were once reasonable become overwhelming.

When we develop expectations, it is very difficult to adjust to actions that reduce what we have come to expect. "Fine—that merely requires an attitude adjustment," you might say. But there's more here. What is being reduced is food for the spirit. Food for the spirit is what allows us to do our best and to be proud of what we do. The people in the Ethiopian village were soon to discover that no more food would be arriving for them. They would either die or have to leave the village that they loved. The same phenomenon occurs in corporations. When food for the spirit is cut off, many people either die on the job or leave the business community that they love.

3. The Aftermath Experience

There is often a collective self-recrimination at the apparent flaws in a relief operation, such as the redundancy and waste that result from the requirements of the emergency. It sounds like "I can't believe this organization could be so disorganized. We need better systems!" To think that, at the height of an emergency, systems can be put into place that could adequately address the multitude of variables that surface is unrealistic. An emergency situation is initially out of control—by definition.

It is important to know that when the self-recrimination begins to appear, it is simply the most appropriate time to realize that the emergency is over and the relief has been provided. Now it is time for long-term development. It is time to look at what systems, designs, and rituals will best help the business to operate optimally in the new world resulting from the changes that occurred during the emergency.

Secondly, there is a collective grief at the loss of a certain spirit and feeling of community that were present during the emergency, brought out because of the crisis. We hear it as "Things just aren't like they used to be. The team spirit, the way we pulled together, is gone. Nobody cares anymore." The unrealistic expectation is that the kind of community that is created through crisis will carry forth beyond the emergency. As Scott Peck writes in *The Different Drum* (1987), community can be created in times other than crisis. But to do that does, in fact, require conscious choice and deliberate hard work.

Conclusion

The effects of spiritual poverty are more subtle than the effects of physical poverty, but they are equally real and debilitating. The losses resulting from the wasting of our spirits, while not as physically apparent as the wasting of our bodies, are greater than we can imagine.

Thus, while relief is critical and essential, it is not sufficient to counteract the effects of poverty—neither the refugee's physical poverty nor the corporate employee's spiritual poverty. The intention of relief is to provide the refugee and the corporate employee with a renewed capability. This capability will allow both to take the step to the next stage—that of development.

The desired results of international development are self-sufficiency of individuals and communities and sustainability of the planetary system. Parallel results in the business context are empowered individuals, teams that are self-managed, and increased profitability of the business system. Initiatives—whether building a learning organization, valuing diversity, or undertaking collaborative organizational design—that support the development of the human spirit reflect organizational opportunities for people to bring more of who they are to the workplace.

Whether it is relief or development that is required, it is important to remember that it is not relationship itself that is the core possibility. Relationship is the *result*—the result of authenticity. Authenticity is the result of tapping the spiritual well, the wisdom within. Therefore, the actual competitive edge is in consciously addressing conditions that result in spiritual poverty within each individual.

The need for relief must be attended to before development can be truly successful. I am reminded of the parable about the student who asks the teacher to teach him. The teacher points to a full cup of tea. He tells the student to pour more tea into the already full cup. Of course, the tea spills over the sides of the cup. The teacher points to this as a metaphor for the student's current ability to learn. First, some of the tea in the cup must be poured out. Providing spiritual relief in organizations is often an activity of emptying the cup, which results in minds and hearts that are open to take in new possibilities about how the workplace can function. Providing relief from fear, anxiety, isolation, apathy, and despair in organizations is a means of preparing ourselves for fuller development.

When we are more authentic, we are capable of creating new solutions and opportunities, of connecting more fully and deeply with each other, of taking more responsibility for the well-being of our businesses, and of becoming more awake to the world in which we live.

Kim McMillen is a consultant in organizational development and change. She considers herself a teacher and philosopher who finds the world of work to be the most challenging place to share what she is learning. Her clients include American Medical International, the Denver Regional Council of Governments, ARC International, and the Center for Quality Schools.

Her articles have appeared in *The New Leaders* business newsletter, *Colorado Lawyer* magazine, and the *Denver Business Journal*.

6

The Workplace as Spiritual Haven

Kim McMillen

Six years ago, I made two major decisions regarding the direction of my life. The first enabled the second, though at the time I did not see that. The first was made consciously, the choice to work for myself, to create my own consulting practice. The second evolved much more subtly and, in reality, was not a choice. Rather, it was a compelling, inner urging so keen that it could not be denied. I had no choice. My soul demanded a commitment and allegiance to my inner psychological and spiritual journey toward wholeness. This became an exploration of the truths of my body, mind, and spirit and a deep surrender to the guidance of my own divine wisdom. I had no idea of the opportunity and challenge, the joy and terror that I was opening myself to.

Throughout this time, I have paid close attention. I knew that I had made choices that allowed me to explore the world of work and the world of my soul simultaneously. I knew that I was learning something to be shared with others. I repeatedly questioned what these two experiences were showing me. Over time, the following ideas took shape:

- This inner transforming imperative of psycho-spiritual growth is part of a mushrooming shift in human consciousness and development now taking place in which our creative capacities and intuitive abilities are being greatly heightened in order to address the plight of our abused and depleted planet.

- The world of work has been a powerful shaper of our privately held values. But now we are hungry for a work that offers a larger sense of meaning and purpose to which we can willingly, even eagerly, commit ourselves, our energy, our time, and our talents. We want a workplace that feeds the spirit as well as the pocketbook.

- Many people, whom I call *spiritual pioneers,* are experiencing an increasing momentum in their transformative shift and are struggling to manage this personal evolution in workplaces uninformed about and unresponsive to their challenging experiences of human expansion.

- A workplace that provides a supportive, informed, accepting perspective and environment—a "spiritual haven" based on compassion, nurturance, and relatedness—could greatly assist this evolutionary process and transform itself in so doing.

- Presently, many spiritual pioneers are choosing to leave businesses that are too restrictive. This is a major loss and disruption not only for the individual, but for business as well.

- As more and more people evolve spiritually and expand consciously, the primary agenda of business will become the reclamation, protection, and preservation of our global environments, systems, and peoples.

Albert Einstein once counseled, "All that is valuable in human society depends upon the opportunity for development accorded to the individual." Spiritual pioneers are poised on the brink of perhaps the most unique opportunity for development in human history. This is the work of the individual journey back to spirit. It has begun. And it is in the world of work that much of this can and should take place.

Inner and Outer Realities

At varying rates of speed, spiritual pioneers are beginning to experience intensifying psychospiritual growth or emergence. Sometimes this is a gradual, manageable experience of change. Sometimes it is rapid, strange, and overwhelming, so that everyday functioning becomes very difficult. This is spiritual emergency or crisis and needs to be understood.

Both experiences lead to wholeness—a reunion of previously abandoned aspects of our souls. Without this wholeness, we will be forever distracted, unable to turn our attention and energy to global healing. We will fail to acquire that larger, mystical awareness of the interconnectedness of life. These are the necessary preparations for the infusion of inspired creativity that we are moving toward. Peter Senge, director of Systems Thinking and the Organizational Learning Program at MIT, calls this larger creativity "metanoia," from the Greek word meaning a transcendent shift beyond the mind, to direct knowing from God. This shift can take place only when a person divests and heals him- or herself of the addictive control and distractions of the ego-mind. Such is the work of the spiritual journey.

This journey starts innocuously enough with a turning inward, a call to solitude, a more ambitious pursuit of self-knowledge, an opening to more conscious awareness, and over time can accelerate and intensify into an extreme purification of body and mind. It is joined by a quickening of spirit and an opening of the heart as the totality of the soul is achieved. Clearly, most people cannot economically afford to set aside earning a living. Yet they will find that they cannot set aside or quiet the soul's call to grow. Somehow, the two must meld. For many, a choice point is near.

Rewards for the Workplace

Companies that choose to provide a spiritual haven will be greatly rewarded, but not without a cost. Creating environments that support the inner spiritual growth of the individual involves disruption, expense, and the introduction of many unknowns, anathemas to the world of business. What I am proposing requires enormous risk and a willingness to gamble courageously. Only businesses which are committed to the transforming principle and priority of full human development will find the courage and faith to carve out the time and means to support these invisible inner evolutions.

The rewards I see are as follows:

- A proliferation of creative input and higher consciousness aimed at serving the good of all humanity and its physical home, the earth. The primary business of business becomes the health and well-being of all our internal and external environments. These larger goals replace the provincial, competitive scramble for market share and power, becoming a true international, collaborative effort.

- As people consciously evolve and truly perceive the interconnectedness of all life, waste, deceit, greed and abuse become intolerable. This leads to a savings in money and resources, an appreciation of diversity, a decrease in conflict, and a return to quality. Caring, respect, and reverence increase.

- More fully evolved and developed human beings create a work force highly attuned to who they are, what their strengths and weaknesses are, and who know their special place and contribution. This means the right person in the right place doing what he or she cares about. Issues of initiative, responsibility, motivation, commitment, and productivity become moot, for these are people who both lead and follow themselves.

- Companies whose economic endeavors include higher ideals and larger purpose naturally and effortlessly attract and keep employees committed to those same ideals.

- With a more nurturing, compassionate environment, a healthier, less stressed work force ensues. Employees bring more energy, effort, and clarity to their jobs, working smarter, more effectively, and with greater satisfaction. Health insurance costs, absenteeism, and enthusiasm are all positively affected.

The Inevitability of Change and Evolution

We humans are creatures of habit. In the past, we have let inertia take over and keep us in place rather than challenging our fears and resistance to change. Today, however, change is not something that we choose or control. It is a given in our lives, and transition is the context of our world. Everywhere we are witnessing the fall of rigid, inhumane institutions and systems. This outer crumbling simply reflects what is happening to human beings on the inside. Overtly or covertly, we are all evolving. It is our birthright. It is going to cause considerable discomfort for many. This is coming to feel like a chasm between personal values and those of the workplace. Increasingly, people are going to find it impossible to hold in place the mask, the facade so long expected and condoned in their working lives.

Deep transformative change means change from the inside out. This does not happen easily; it is often painful and usually requires a catalyst. Presently, we have a workplace built on values of law, form, control, competition, and a work force seeking compassion, meaningful work, and spiritual nourishment. The friction between the two is building, change is in the air, and the catalysts are present.

Transformative Catalysts

There are two invisible catalysts that exert themselves energetically. The first is higher, cosmic, or Christ consciousness energy. The second is kundalini energy, long understood and revered in Hindu and other Eastern traditions, but much more rarely encountered in our control-oriented Western cultures.

The cosmic energy affects the electromagnetic field surrounding the body. It is beginning to affect greater numbers of human beings more directly as they open themselves receptively to their spiritual evolution. This energy, with its higher vibratory rate, can be felt distinctly in the body and catalyzes a shift to higher consciousness as people liberate themselves from domination by the fearful, controlling ego-mind. The kundalini energy is a sometimes gradual, sometimes very sudden awakening on a cellular level in the body, with a cleansing or purifying electrical energy moving up the spine and circulating eventually through the brain.

Possible Experiences of the Spiritual Pioneer

Mentally, the predominant experience is a feeling of loss of control and the fear that it engenders. Left-brain, linear, logical, analytical thinking becomes elusive and at times impossible. Memory, decision making, sense of purpose, motivation, initiative, linear sense of time, and the desire to relate and/or communicate with others can disappear as one's inner focus takes over. A sense of loss can predominate physically as well. Sleep patterns and duration can be greatly affected. The appetite may greatly increase or decrease and become very selective. Weight loss is common. Deep fatigue and lethargy occur frequently. The heart may race, pound, or lose its rhythm.

These physical sensations ebb and flow and, combined with the mental experiences, can be overstimulating, disconcerting, and anxiety producing, making concentration very difficult and leaving one with a sense of disconnection to previously known reality.

In the emotional realm, volatility and intensity occur in most cases. The unconscious may deliver up strong doses of memories. Emotional states change abruptly and are often extremely intense. Swings between polarized emotions are common, leaving the person feeling chaotic internally. Rigid patterns of behavior and ego boundaries begin to crumble, leaving one feeling highly vulnerable.

Spiritually, polarized swings may also occur, from mystical or unitive states, where the sacred dimensions are glimpsed, to the arid "dark night of the soul" where all connection with God disappears. Psychic experiences of telepathy, clairvoyance, clairaudience, and visions may begin or increase. Linear time may cease to exist in ecstatic episodes that defy description. Bliss, peace, deep gratitude, and awe may be felt, as well as tremendous fear of the awesomeness of the Divine. Often a strong preference for silence and an inward listening stance may develop as one's receptivity to communion with God deepens. Because of the transcendent nature of some of these experiences, one may have real difficulty relating to and caring about the more mundane side of life.

What I have described sounds overwhelming and can be, especially if not understood. Fortunately, these experiences do not all occur simultaneously; they move in cycles, with periods of integration before the next wave of energetic input of increased vibrational frequency. This shifting back and forth from outer work to inner work can be disruptive and confusing. What the person is doing inwardly—surrendering old habits and belief systems, emptying oneself in order to receive from a universal source—the workplace must do as well if it is committed to becoming a spiritual haven. And this commitment is fueled by faith and trust only. There is no way to see this process, to measure it, evaluate it, or put a form to it. It has a life of its own and cannot be manipulated or controlled. This will constantly call into question the commitment of the spiritual pioneer and the organization. To remain steady, to persevere in the face of the unknown, is an enormous challenge to both.

What Do Spiritual Pioneers Need?

Mentally, spiritual pioneers need to be free of expectations. Trying to perform or generating the will to perform can actually exacerbate the anxiety that is often prevalent during these transitional times.

Emotionally, spiritual pioneers need the freedom to honor what uniquely makes them feel safe. This may include appropriate counseling, creative outlets that encourage the expression of feelings, keeping a journal about their process, or frequent contact with supportive, nonjudgmental friends or family members.

Physically, they need to learn what soothes and calms the energetic impact on the body. There are many forms of body work that assist by releasing blocked energy in muscles and tissues. Many people respond well to soaking in water, being outdoors, moderate exercise, especially in a natural setting, and simple gardening and cleaning chores. Often people need physical contact, such as being held, and hugged.

Spiritually, people need increased amounts of solitude to provide a time of receptivity to the inflow of spiritual quickening and inspiration. Meditation, prayer, inner listening, and reflection become a means of nourishment at this time. Spiritual guidance from a teacher or spiritual community that understands this process may also be advisable.

Creating a Spiritual Haven

To create a realistic spiritual haven, it is essential that everyone in an organization has a clear understanding of what a spiritual haven is meant to be. First and foremost, it is a program of support and education. It is not a therapeutic program and does not replace one. Second, it is support for a process of growth, not a process of illness. Finally, it is a compassionate response that enables spiritual pioneers to more fully live their transformative process with integrity, having to neither repress nor deny their experience.

There are no formulas for creating spiritual havens. Each workplace would create its own to suit its special needs and constraints. It would be wise to use input from those it would serve. The following are cornerstones to strive for:

Flexibility. This is an experience with no predictability. It comes and goes in varying cycles of intensity and duration. Ideally, spiritual pioneers need to be able to control their ability to step out of normal work routines and roles in response to their inner needs. To be able to leave the work site, to get outdoors, to reduce stimulation and pressure when necessary would all be appropriate.

Support. A cadre of trained volunteer companions from within the organization could be formed. The companion's role is to be available when fear and isolation anxieties are extreme, to be a listener, to provide logistical and scheduling assistance when requested, and to help the pioneer make contact with appropriate community resources, such as physicians, mental health workers, teachers, support groups, and body workers.

A consultant to the program who has experienced a spiritual emergence and can guide and educate the organization and its employees at the outset of the development of a spiritual haven is recommended. This person could also provide counseling and educational support to individuals when appropriate.

Spiritual pioneers who find themselves in a work environment that is not willing to develop a spiritual haven could initiate a support group of fellow pioneers to assist each other in many of the same ways suggested here.

An additional means of support would be short-term housing alternatives. People in spiritual transition often need time out from spouses or living partners, who may feel threatened by the upheaval and changes taking place in their loved one.

Education. An on-site resource center and library, available to all employees, spiritual pioneers, volunteers, and family members would be valuable. Listings of local support services should also be provided, along with the address and telephone number of the Spiritual Emergence Network (SEN): 5905 Soquel Avenue, Suite #650, Soquel, CA 95073, phone (408) 464-8261. SEN is an international organization that offers referral services and educational support to those going through a spiritual transformation, the professionals working with them, and their families and friends.

Solitude and Slow Time. This experience is one of intense, internal stimulation. Often, being alone is the best course of action. Small, private rooms in the workplace to be used as retreat spaces would be most helpful. Permission to move at a slower pace is critical to enable people to process, absorb, and integrate the variety of experiences that they may be encountering. What appears to be "doing nothing" on the outside may actually be important "work" taking place on the inside.

Safety and Simplicity. Safety can be provided through the attitudes of co-workers—an understanding and acceptance of the vulnerability that most spiritual pioneers feel. Often, even the simplest demands can be overwhelming, because linear thinking and the will to take action can disappear. To be aware of this and provide support in simplifying all sorts of the everyday mechanisms of work life would be appropriate assistance.

Cornerstones of a Spiritual Haven

1. Flexibility: acknowledgment of "inner" needs and suspension of work pressures as needed
2. Support: people and systems that are available if requested by the pioneer
3. Education: available sources of information about the spiritual emergence process
4. Solitude: support for "quiet time," privacy, and permission to slow down as needed
5. Safety and simplicity: understanding and acceptance by fellow workers, without criticism

---

A New Foundation of Values

None of this will be possible without a radical shift in the values from which businesses form and conduct themselves. The following values require a bold leap of faith which can move the world of work into a major shift of consciousness.

- Human development and evolution become the primary measure of success, replacing acquisition of power, control, and out-of-scale profit.

- Larger purpose and the higher good, when given top priority, naturally guide economic endeavor to positive outcomes.

- Compassion, nurturance, receptivity, and harmony take their rightful and *equal* place alongside the achievement and action.

- Creative expression and service become the raison d'être for work.

- Introversion, that psychological preference for the inner world over the external world which naturally accompanies a deeper spiritual search, becomes understood, accepted, and appreciated.

- Spiritual emergence and transformation are seen as a natural, healthy growth process to be honored and included in the world of work.

- The inner authority and wisdom of the individual, which become acutely more attuned and refined during this process, are respected by all, regardless of title or role.

- The "dark" or "shadow" side of people and processes, which includes destruction, fear, and not knowing, is recognized as a necessary counterbalancing force in people and the processes of creativity, transformation, and achievement.

- Fear, so large a factor in any transformative process and certainly present in the business world, is acknowledged and managed maturely so that it no longer manipulates decision makers into grasping at short-term solutions and gain while ignoring long-term impacts and the larger good.

• Trust, patience, and perseverance with all of the above become the context in which business is conducted. The search for security is abandoned in order to allow this new set of values to bear the fruits of quality, productivity, financial health, and stability.

The Trappist monk Thomas Merton once said, "The greatest human temptation is to settle for too little." We have settled for too little for too long. We have sometimes let our work be petty and small and unnourishing of our souls. It is time to change that. We presently have the opportunity to transform our work, the workplace, and ourselves. In so doing, we reclaim the depths and complexity of our being and the magnificence of our home, the earth. Let us begin. Who will make those first leaps of faith?

Jacqueline Haessly is the author of several books and more than one hundred articles, which have been published in more than thirty national and international publications. Her book *Learning to Live Together* provides practical ideas for incorporating values, shaping attitudes, and developing skills necessary to create peace within the family, the community, and the world. She offers consultation, lectures, workshops, and retreats to local and national business, educational, and community organizations. She is currently pursuing doctoral studies at the Union Institute in Cincinnati, Ohio.

A more detailed version of this essay, including a six-part "Values Checklist," can be ordered for U.S.$10.00, prepaid, including postage and handling, directly from Peace Talks Publications, 2437 North Grant Boulevard., Milwaukee, WI 53210. No phone orders, please.

7

A Quest for Quality: Values for the Global Marketplace

Jacqueline Haessly

Albert Einstein stated that the splitting of the atom changed everything except our way of thinking. Today, much of corporate thinking is oriented toward reaching or remaining in a preeminent position, toward maintaining that competitive edge, over all others. Jane Addams, the social reformer who won the Nobel Peace Prize in 1931, reminds us that the good that we secure for ourselves is only as strong as the good that we secure for all. Reports of ever-increasing outbreaks of family, neighborhood, and urban violence and scattered international violence— an escalation of terrorist activity around the world, hostage taking, and warfare—testify that the good has not yet been secured for all and provide constant reminders of the impact of social unrest on our corporate as well as our personal and family lives. Our children, the hope and promise for the future, are the greatest victims of this social unrest. *Fortune* magazine devoted its entire August 1992 issue to this topic. "Children in Crisis: A Special Report" provided compelling reasons for reexamining our values and the corporate policies and practices that they inform.

Corporate decision makers who plan for company success in the 1990s and beyond face a critical challenge—to examine and, if necessary, change traditional ways of thinking. I wish to explore these paradigms and values as they apply to business in today's global marketplace. We begin with an exploration of the concept of values for global health and wholeness. Six values that seem paramount for our corporate and global future are examined in greater depth. For each value, I include thought-provoking questions for personal and corporate reflection. I close with a modest proposal for a new interpretation of the phrase "quest for quality" for today's global marketplace.

New Paradigms

The challenge that faces those wishing to pick from the array of goods and services, resources and profits available in the global marketplace is a challenge of values. Every person, every business, every government operates on a set of values. Our challenge is to determine which values will enable us to move into the twenty-first century in a manner that will both promote the success of our business *and* enhance the quality of life for all. To meet this challenge, our paradigms must change to reflect a new way of thinking about our community, our world, and our company's place within it. This global market-place calls us to discover and develop a whole new way of relating with others who share space with us on this small planet that we each call home.

If it is true that the good that we secure for ourselves is only as strong as the good that we secure for all, what does this tell us about the decisions that corporate managers must make today for our corporate future? Our children's future? Our community's future? Our global future? Is there a relationship, and, if so, what is it? What does our quest for quality really mean in this increasingly globally interdependent world? In an era of rapidly escalating population growth, global turmoil, and limited natural resources, what values are most important to ensure that *all* of humanity has access to the essentials for human dignity and life?

This is the question that Saul Mendlowitz (1975) and his associates from the Institute for World Order pondered as early as 1966, when the World Order Models Project was formed. They began with questions about war and peace and soon realized that while peace and the elimination of war might be of concern to the industrialized world, economic well-being and social justice have a much higher priority in less developed countries. Indeed, for some, these matters were seen as part of the definition of the problem of war and therefore held the solution to war prevention. Three key questions emerged: (1) What *values* are necessary in order to create a just and preferred world by the year 1999? (2) What *decisions* do we make today to reflect those values? (3) What *actions* do we take today in order to move toward the achievement of a just world order by the twenty-first century?

Six Values for the Global Marketplace

For our purposes, we will refer to values for the global marketplace as ecological balance, social responsibility, political participation, economic transformation, global spirituality, and a world of peace without armed conflict. These "world order" values are considered imperative by Mendlowitz and his colleagues if humanity is to survive on this planet into the twenty-first century.

Each of these values has special significance for those of us involved with or concerned about corporate enterprises. Let us now explore each of these values and the questions they raise in greater depth. The following reflections, grouped according to the six world order values, offer a starting place for personal and corporate education, reflection, and discussion. Implementation of decisions that reflect these values will promote human dignity and enhance your own company's quest for quality.

121

Ecological Balance

Our earth is a fragile planet that all people everywhere call home. Life on this planet will survive only if we eliminate or reduce exploitation of nonrenewable resources, environmental pollution, nuclear warfare, and other threats to this fragile ecosystem.

According to Mendlowitz, even if all other human problems, including racial and civil violence, social, economic and political injustices, and warfare, were resolved, life itself might not survive far into the twenty-first century unless we implement environmentally sound practices today. We cannot continue to deplete the rain forests and other life-sustaining resources of the earth, diminish nonrenewable resources, overgraze or overdevelop arable land, pollute the air, land, and water, and still provide for our children's future. Thus, humanity is urged to act with promptness to halt the pollution of the environment and return it to a state of ecological balance in order to protect this fragile ecosystem, which has given us life and which continues to nurture and sustain us.

Our greatest challenge is to work cooperatively with others from diverse disciplines and countries, seeking solutions and making decisions that ensure a healthy environment for all the world's children. In response to this challenge, a growing number of corporations, including cosmetic firms that use natural ingredients and refrain from animal testing, fast-food establishments that use recyclable packaging, and companies that harvest renewable products from the rain forests while leaving the trees intact are seeking to address issues of resource conservation and ecological balance in their policies and strategies for growth.

Corporate leaders who are concerned about values for ecological balance seek answers to questions regarding the quality of their product of service. Their questions, however, will also address such issues as how in an environmentally sound way to access raw materials; use renewable and nonrenewable resources; manufacture, process, and transport the product; dispose of manufacturing waste; maintain an effective monitoring system; promote corporate and citizen compliance with government regulations; provide environmental education, research, and development opportunities for staff and community; assess the impact of corporate work on the environment; and make a commitment to a renewal of the earth and implement policies and practices that reflect that commitment.

Social Responsibility

All people everywhere have a right to belong, to feel safe, and to be treated with dignity and respect. All people everywhere have a right to equal opportunity and access to food, shelter, health care, education, work, and family regardless of their age, sex, race, ethnic or national origin, political or religious persuasion, economic background, or lifestyle.

Corporate decision makers who value social responsibility recognize that people have a right to live with family members in community with others where they can develop positive self-esteem and experience a sense of belonging and inclusion that fosters personal, family, and community safety and where their sense of connectedness to others is nurtured. Most importantly, they work to establish public and corporate policy and practice that will reduce discrimination and segregation in education, housing, employment, health care, and other arenas of human need and that promote equality of opportunity to all. It also recognizes that we are all called to care for the children of the planet and to provide for their emotional, physical, spiritual, and moral well-being.

Issues that corporate leaders might consider regarding implementation of policies that enhance values of social responsibility include cooperative rather than competitive thinking and acting; equality of opportunity in employment practices; equitable access to products and services; responsible advertising, marketing, and sales practices; access to education, housing, health, and child-care needs; respect for cultural diversity and life-style choices, and mutuality; and the elimination of human exploitation, including all forms of sexual exploitation, of women, men, and children.

123

It is important for corporate leaders to examine policies that affect these social issues, either for staff or for the community in which their business operates. Companies that provide child-care for employees, training programs for school drop-outs and ex-offenders, or mentoring and educational programs in the communities where they do business reflect a corporate commitment to social responsibility.

Economic Transformation

All people everywhere have the right to adequate reimbursement for meaningful work and a right to share in access to and distribution of the goods and resources of the earth.

A value for economic transformation addresses the growing economic disparity between rich and poor in our own country and between developed countries and less-developed countries around the world. Patricia Mische, writing in the fall 1988 issue of *Breakthrough* (published by Global Education Associates), reminds us that *eco* means "house," and thus *economics*, which now refers to the production, distribution and consumption of goods and services, originally meant the management of a household.

A glance at the evening news would suggest that the condition of our global household is in serious need of care. Its resources have not been managed very well for the good of the inhabitants who share life in that household, our world. Development programs, world trade agreements and the United Nations' New International Economic Order are just three of the hundreds of attempts that have been made in the last twenty years to address this growing global problem. Yet, as Gita Zen (1990) reminds us, development programs have, in many cases, led to greater economic hardship as women and children have been denied access to the very water, food, and fuel on which they have traditionally depended for their community needs.

There is growing economic disparity between the more prosperous countries of the Northern Hemisphere and the growing numbers of people in South and Central America,

124

Africa and the subcontinent of India who live in economic misery. There is also a widening gap between rich and poor in our own country, resulting in widespread hunger, homelessness and premature deaths from lack of adequate food, health care, and the violence that erupts when people are caught in a cycle of poverty and hopelessness. Religious leaders, community and government leaders alike have raised questions about this life-threatening disparity.

Economic transformation occurs when those who have access to and control of the financial resources of a family, a community, or a corporation recognize their mutual interdependence and use these resources in ways that foster equality and mutuality among people. Among these are companies that affirm that capital and labor are equally essential for the success of a company and are building economic parity into the corporate financial picture.

Issues for corporate consideration regarding values for economic transformation include the written and unwritten hiring and promotion policies of the company and its impact in both our own country and other countries; pricing policies for goods and services; a just return to investors; financial regulations; and investment and trade policies. Other issues for corporate consideration include ownership and access to raw materials and natural resources; the complex issues of job security (whose jobs? where? and at what cost to the environment?); equitable distribution of the wealth in the world; debt reduction; and strategies and risks necessary to effect change.

A sampling of businesses that have incorporated values for economic transformation into corporate policy include lending institutions that offer homeowner counseling programs and provide mortgages to low income residents of the community; companies that reinvest in the community in which they do business; companies whose shareholders, managers, and labor force share equally in profits and losses; and companies that return a percentage of profits to environmental, peace, and social action causes.

Political Participation

All people everywhere have a right to participate in the decisions that affect their lives. This also means that they have a right to adequate access to accurate information from effective education and an uncensored media in order to make informed decisions.

Whenever people are excluded from decisions that affect their lives, the danger of political injustice arises. Such injustice exists to some degree in all countries. Corporate and government leaders routinely make decisions that have an impact on the lives of a people, often without their direct involvement in or even knowledge of, the issue to be decided. What is the impact of these decisions on the daily lives of the people who work in the firm or in whose city, state, or country the company is located?

Other issues include management style, clash of political or economic ideologies, cross-cultural and cross-national cooperation, international agreements, self-determination, and equitable access to the resources of the earth. How and when do corporate leaders and the press provide enough information so that people can make informed choices about their work and their future? These are some of the challenges raised by those who value political participation. Today, large and small companies integrate political participation into their corporate structure, inviting employees at all levels to participate in decisions regarding such topics as wages, profits and losses of the company, products to be manufactured, and corporate presence in other countries (Coleman 1991).

Global Spirituality

All people have a right to their own religious heritage and a right to celebrate the diverse ways in which they express their unity with other people, creation, and a spiritual being.

A global spirituality respects the diverse ways in which people express their connectedness with others on this planet and with a spiritual or god force that gives their life meaning. A global spirituality reflects an attitude that values the sacredness of life in all its diverse expressions. Thus, all life is treated with dignity and deep respect. A global spirituality calls forth a sense of integrity in one's life, one's relationships, and one's work; a sense of centeredness and purpose that grounds one's direction in life; a sense of compassion—with passion—for the suffering of others, whoever they may be and wherever they may live; a sense of empathy with the experience of another; a sense of responsibility that leads one to action on behalf of oneself or another; and a sense of wonder, creativity, and playfulness with which we celebrate our existence.

Issues for reflection and discussion regarding values of global spirituality in the corporate setting include a recognition that religious practices and customs differ from religious group to religious group and even within any one religious tradition. Does our business reflect a sensitivity to the religious customs of the people and culture of the area where we are doing business? Should it? These are questions that affect marketing, advertising, work hours, products or services offered, use or desecration of land or artifacts, and implementation of company policies. What should our corporate policy be regarding values for global spirituality? What economic, political, and social risks does this entail for our company? These important questions require special sensitivity to diverse personal and cultural beliefs. How we address them will have a significant impact on our corporate well-being.

World Peace Without Armed Conflict

People have a right to have their own legitimate needs and wants respected and a responsibility to respect the legitimate needs and wants of others. When conflicts arise, people have a right to resolve these conflicts in ways that don't cause harm to themselves or others.

A world of peace without armed conflict suggests that we as humans can discover new and effective ways to resolve conflicts between ourselves and others *without* use of violence. It's been said that the history of the world is a record of its wars. However, in a few brief years in terms of the history of the world, groups that once were enemies and used weapons against each other now consider themselves allies and even friends. We *can* learn to live without an identified "enemy." As we approach the twenty-first century, it seems important to reclaim our history of nonviolent responses to, and peaceful resolution of, conflicts.

This calls for a new way of thinking, a new paradigm, one that embraces a vision of negotiation, consensus decision making, and win-win solutions to critical economic, political, and social problems, both at home and abroad. It further suggests that we can continue to expand our abilities to embrace others into the ever-widening circle of people we include as family and friends in our cities, countries, and continents and ultimately, our new global village.

Today we observe nation-states that once engaged in armed conflict using conferences and courts to resolve disputes. We have local, state, and national mediation centers and courts to help resolve intergovernmental disputes regarding issues of land and resource use, access, safety, and pollution. The mechanisms are in place, tried and effective. The need is to translate these working mechanisms to the global sphere and to embrace a commitment among government, corporate, and community leaders from all nations to ensure that these mechanisms work.

Questions for corporate consideration include the relationship between our development and investment policies, self-determination, management styles, cross-cultural agreements, current trade or lending practices, political unrest within and between countries, and international conflicts.

Facing The Challenges

How corporate leaders integrate these six values into the realities of daily business decisions and limited financial resources and still succeed in these last years of the twentieth century is a challenge facing all companies. Is this within the realm of reality or do the values posed by the World Order Models Project speak of a utopia? According to futurist Willis Harman and IBM executive John Hormann (1991), writing in their book *Creative Work: The Constructive Role of Business in a*

Transforming Society, "the global dilemma which faces corporate decision-makers can be simply stated. *Of the easily imaginable paths of global development, those that appear to be economically feasible do not look to be ecologically and socially plausible, and those that appear ecologically feasible and humanely desirable do not seem economically and politically feasible"* (emphasis theirs). Yet as Coleman (1991) reminds us, "the economies of entire nations depend upon the emerging creative capacities of their people [to effect change]. The overall quality of a nation's life hinges on the application of intelligence and wisdom to resolve problems at work."

It is the belief of a growing number of people that businesses can meet this challenge. Today, an increasing number of businesses are basing decisions for the future on values for social responsibility and global wholeness. Anita Roddick, 1987 British Business Woman of the Year and founder and president of The Body Shop International, develops and sells cosmetics for the whole family. The company incorporates dimensions of all six values in all phases of its work. According to Coleman, Roddick believes that a company can both make money and make ethical and moral decisions. Although the company enjoys a 50 percent annual growth rate, Roddick puts it this way: "I don't want our success to be measured only by financial yardsticks, or by our distribution or number of shops. What I want to be celebrated for—and it's going to be tough in a business environment—is how good we are to our employees and how we benefit our community. It's a different bottom line" (Coleman 1991).

Today, the growing number of companies that actively promote socially responsible criteria in their decision-making processes include Johnson & Johnson, Family Pastimes, Quad Graphics, Ben & Jerry's Homemade, Europe Through the Back Door Travel Agency, and The Body Shop International, among others. All are recognized as strong, financially viable companies.

Criteria for socially responsible decision making differ among companies. For some, the criteria are environmental; for

129

some, racial or gender equality in the work place; and for others, divestment in South Africa, nuclear issues, or military involvement in weapons research or production. While it is imperative that each company define its own criteria, I believe that criteria for socially responsible decision making must ultimately reflect all six values for global wholeness. Only then can we truly effect a "quest for quality" in the global marketplace.

A Quest for Quality with a Difference

Quality is a watchword for businesses seeking to survive the tumultuous business climate of the nineties. We have "quality control," "quality management," and "quality circles," each aimed at developing a better product or service, improving worker, customer, or client satisfaction, and ultimately increasing corporate share of the local, regional, or global marketplace. Business leaders who are on a quest for quality are challenged to look beyond the traditional interpretations of that word to examine a deeper dimension of its meaning. They are encouraged to embark on a quest for quality that will move us into the twenty-first century in a manner that will both promote the success of our business and enhance the quality of life for all.

This "quest for quality" challenges us to *question* interpretations of events and experiences and traditional ways of thinking and doing business. It calls us to *understand* the connectedness between government and corporate policies and their impact on people in our community and our world and the implications of our decisions for today's and future generations. It urges us to *educate* ourselves and our young, to respect and celebrate diversity, and educate ourselves and others about the challenges that we face and the opportunities that they present. It summons us to *secure*

QUEST for Quality
Q *question*
U *understand*
E *educate*
S *secure*
T *treasure*

130

personal, family, and community safety for our young and not so young, political safety for those who differ from us and to secure peace in the world for our own and future generations. Lastly, our quest invites us to *treasure:* our life, our children, our families, our community, our earth, and all the gifts and resources that it provides for us. If we follow this quest, we will surely reflect quality in our work and in our world.

Those involved with the World Order Models Project suggested that there is no one way to achieve a just and preferred world by the year 2000. Each corporation, whether large or small, within each culture and each country, must work out the dynamics of implementing these world order values within the context of their own experience, keeping in mind the challenge to build together toward a preferred and just world future, a world of global wholeness. These issues are suggested as starting points for leaders in business, education, religious and social institutions, and government to explore together from the vantage point of their own unique economic, political, social, and cultural heritage.

Companies engaged in a "quest for quality" in products, service, and employee and community relationships that also incorporate values for global wholeness into their decision-making process, *can* make a difference. Talking and acting together we can choose for global wholeness. Some have shown the way. Let us be the voices that encourage others to follow, because we each have an investment in the future of this small planet that gave us life and that we each call home.

Part Three

Creating Networks, Support Systems, and a Spirit of Community

Helping Your Dream Job Find You
Jan Nickerson

Organizational Renewal Through a Hunger for Meaning
Anne Lippitt Rarich

Chaos to Community: One Company's Journey of Transformation
Jeanne Borei

A World We've Only Dreamed Of
Hope Xaviermineo

Historically, women have gathered to support each other, sometimes by plan—quilting bees, weddings, "socials"—and other times out of necessity—the birth of a child, a death, or some other family emergency. That desire for connection continues in the workplace as well where many women, and men, feel isolated and alone. During turbulent times, this isolation can create a climate of pure survival when moving forward requires an openness to change. This part gives us glimpses of new ways of making connections that nourish us and support our personal and professional growth.

Jan Nickerson created a job-search support network as she pursued a career change. Like Kathleen Keating, she used gardening as a metaphor to help her better understand her job search process, enabling her to persevere with the process rather than taking her search to a premature conclusion. We've all heard the story about the gardener who planted the seeds and then kept digging them up to see whether they had sprouted. It requires patience to allow an idea to mature and develop, and it takes time and care to prepare the soil in which to grow an idea or project. Patience allowed Jan's "dream" job to unfold in magical ways.

In the process of working to change a Fortune 100 company where she worked, Anne Rarich says she found herself "caught up in the very culture I wanted to change." In response, she entered a time of profound personal growth that enabled her to bring a new perspective to others in the company. "For renewal to occur in an individual, an organization, or a community," she says, "the decision to change and the actions that result in renewal must occur inside each individual." She helped to facilitate the creation of networks among core groups in the company that alleviated much of the tension and "dis-ease" among employees.

Jeanne Borei, after a profound personal experience of working in "community," saw the benefit of applying the same techniques and processes to her company. The approach they used is "community-building," described by Dr. M. Scott Peck in *The Different Drum*. Her story is not only instructive but unique in that, according to Peck, hers is the only company to date to involve every employee in this process.

When Hope Xaviermineo's life was changed radically by a devastating accident, her need for a new way of seeing life was critical. In spite of predictions that she would never walk again, she overcame all obstacles and found perfect health by holding a vision of health and wholeness. She believes that if we can collectively hold a vision of perfect health, peace, and beauty for our planet earth, we can create "A World We've Only Dreamed Of."

Jan Nickerson is a senior financial executive. Her credentials include an M.B.A. degree from Cornell University, a CPA position with Arthur Andersen & Company, and twenty years of corporate financial management with high-growth or rapidly changing businesses. Her most recent employer, Loyalty Management Group, Inc., has grown from 6 people when she joined the firm to more than 150 employees in preparation for its first year of operating its Air Miles programs, which is expected to exceed $100 million in revenue.

Nickerson's vision is that men and women realize their choices in balancing family, self, career, and community without compromise. Nicknamed "Fireball," she is an active member of the Boston Chapter of the World Business Academy. She is also active in the Organization Transformation Network, New England Businesses for Social Responsibility, Cornell's Council for Women, her local Unitarian church, and her three-generational family. She is currently developing practical and inspirational materials to assist others in their job searches.

8

Helping Your Dream Job Find You

Jan Nickerson

For eighteen years in the corporate world, I viewed men and women as people, without relating specifically to an individual's gender. During a recent transition between jobs, I learned the rich distinctions between feminine and masculine energy. I discovered how women had entered the "man's world" of business in large enough numbers to start integrating their feminine style into the workplace. I learned how important the balance of feminine and masculine energy is—both within myself and in our workplaces and communities. I've loved meeting men who have given themselves permission to discover, grow, and share their own feminine side. My career search story is about how I integrated feminine approaches with the masculine skills I had already mastered.

When I was a seventeen-year-old hotel management trainee, disgruntled for being assigned to the housekeeping ranks of an overstaffed summer resort, my dad asked me, "Since you're going to manage people in the future, what can you learn from this experience that will have the housekeepers in your hotel loving their work?" I turned that job into a game of fun, efficiency, and pride in my work and a "promotion" to the reservations staff. I've sought and found the opportunities in the problems of each job since. I've always based major decisions on how I will be shaped by the experience.

Like a Garden

I liken my career search to gardening. I had seen others go into any garden and pick whatever was blooming, often the first flower they saw, often without apparent regard for whether it was a weed, an annual, a biennial, or a perennial. I turned the soil of my garden. I fertilized and sowed it. I planted many seeds—but only of the varieties I wanted in my garden. I watered and nurtured my garden, in the beginning with only the faith that something was growing. And then the garden started to blossom—one plant after another, and another. I would be tempted to pick one when another, more beautiful would appear. And then finally, three exquisite plants bloomed at once.

While it may sound as though my search has been a well-planned project with overwhelming effort, it did not occur that way. Keeping sight of the *whole* kept me flexible and guided me through the process. My search occurred "in the moment," day after day, doing what seemed most appropriate and interesting at that time. What made the difference is that I had faith in my vision of my "dream job."

Seasons

I turned the soil of my garden. I fertilized and sowed it. I watered and nurtured my garden in the beginning with only the faith that something was invisibly growing. And then the garden started to blossom.

The search process was an evolutionary one. When people asked what position I was looking for, it didn't feel right to respond with a singular answer. It felt better to say, "My current thinking is..." or "I'm in an exploratory stage. I know the following qualities will be valued..."

138

I applied the classic product life-cycle concepts to my search process. Like any product in a company, my search evolved through the stages of creating, building, stabilizing, and reaping. Using the garden metaphor, the stages of my process were tilling, sowing, tending, and reaping.

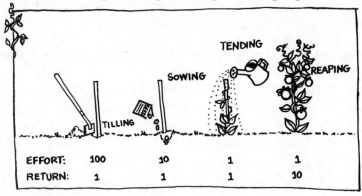

Had I not recognized these stages, I might have invalidated my low yield ratio at the beginning of my search by comparing it to the high-yield ratio of my performance in my previous position, which was in the reaping stage. And by recognizing the more mature stages of my family and support network, I could count on their nurturance without the high level of effort that my new search would demand.

Tilling

I readied the soil of my garden, without which the seeds could not have grown. I turned the soil, aerating the packed, used earth. Last year's growth became a rich compost.

While I was on maternity leave, family and Christmas took priority over my intentions to refocus my career. I resolved to be well on my way to passion in my career in 1990. I had been back on the job for two weeks when the CEO sadly told me that because of our division downsizing, my job required only the power of a popgun and I was a twelve-gauge. My job was eliminated.

139

I Planted My Feet on the Ground

I was advised to spend the evening letting all my negative emotions out. When I said, "But I don't have any," my adviser replied, "Make some up." I spent the evening looking for negative stuff to release, priming the pump by "faking it." That was hard. I've always been optimistic by nature. For me, *there are no problems; just opportunities.* However, I took the advice. After I felt the feelings that were there, I found that my voice changed when I spoke of my past employment and my future dream career. Before, there had been an edge of complaint in my voice—perhaps even an air of victimization. Now my voice came from deep within my body, not from my head. Now my voice could fully express the freedom that I felt to explore and create my future.

I spent my last month on the job wrapping up and reassigning my CFO responsibilities before I bade my final farewell to the hundreds of people with whom I'd worked for the past twelve years.

My husband John and I projected our income and expenses for the next year. We identified our cash reserves and assets that could be converted into cash. I applied for unemployment, which would generate some income over the coming year. We identified lines of credit—with credit cards, banks, and family. We felt comfortable that we could make it for a year. The investment of time and money now would yield for a lifetime my ability to contribute, feel satisfaction, have financial stability, and express passion in my career.

I Cultivated

As in my working career, my family support structure was solidly in place. My husband has always supported me in fulfilling myself. My mother lives with us, doing what she loves best—caring for family, including our daughters, Jamie, then four, and Jenna, our infant. Their love was essential to my success.

My first day "out" was serendipitously spent at the first Boston meeting of the World Business Academy. Fifteen executives, facilitated by Willis Harman, shared a common commitment to a positive global future. For perhaps the first time, I heard others articulate my own unspoken thoughts and feelings. Then I joined a women's group workshop and focused on the distinctions between masculine and feminine energy. I joined Executive Moms, which grew in one year to fifty women who were both mothers and executives. Our business connections were valuable but secondary to our bonding. Where else could I share my exhilaration of multiple dream jobs developing? I also benefited from going to a spiritual learning center whose gentle, receptive, and enlightening energy attracts both women and men. I applied my belief in management coaching to my career search and enrolled the support of two coaches, Sydney Rice and Rondalyn Whitney.

Search as a Full-Time Job

I regarded my search as a full-time job. I had business cards printed up. I dressed in clothes appropriate to the day's activities. I arrived at the office or a breakfast meeting by 8 A.M., experiencing the ritual of leaving home and entering my office. Two or three evenings a week, I attended a seminar or business forum that appealed to me and to the kind of people with whom I would enjoy working. Each day, I assessed my priorities, noted my energy level, and planned my day to support my intentions. I set strategic goals and tactical objectives (for instance, meet with five new people this week). I declared my objectives to my coaches; I knew they would support me in achieving them.

As my search carried beyond the term of our financial comfort, the temptation to accept any offer became strong. Had I invested too much to accept mediocre returns? Or perhaps I was "determined to be starved before I was hungry," as Thoreau so well put it. The truth is, I believed that my dream job would find me.

SOWING

EFFORT: 10
RETURN: 1

Sowing the Seeds

I planted many seeds—but only the varieties I wanted in my garden.

As I became ready to move through my transition, Rondalyn gave me Danaan Parry's (1991) "Fear of Transformation":

> *Sometimes I feel that my life is a series of trapeze swings. I'm either hanging on to a trapeze bar swinging along or for a few moments in my life, I'm hurtling across space in between trapeze bars…. [Each time I let go,] I am filled with terror. It doesn't matter that in all my previous hurtles across the void of knowing, I have always made it… I have noticed that, in our culture, this transition zone is looked upon as a "nothing," a no-place between places…. What a waste! I have a sneaking suspicion that the transition zone is the only real thing, and the bars are illusions we dream up to avoid the void, where the real change, the real growth occurs for us…. Hurtling through the void, we just may learn how to fly.*

Every time I read this, I am reminded of the times my fear of failing has proved to be unjustified. I am inspired to let go, not for what's next, but to be in that enlightening and terrifying space in between. I can feel my heart enlarge and my feminine courage grow. I chose to "learn to fly" during my transition, to reach out and take risks. The size of the risks grew as I learned from the first tiny ones.

This transitional period was a rich time to learn skills or insights that couldn't be learned while employed or hanging on to a trapeze bar. Hanging on to the bar is itself distracting and hides what can be seen only from mid-flight.

I had let my network know that I was looking for a CFO position in a small to mid-sized business. I assessed the values and organizational culture myself until one day a wise new friend remarked, "Sounds like a pretty typical strategy; I imagine you're finding pretty typical jobs." The light went on. I was not interested in any "typical" job. I let go and flew into the space of expressing myself *my* way.

I was clear about my vision—it would source my career with passion. I began with an assessment of "Who am I now?" from which to project the transition toward who I would be. Assessment activities balanced with visioning activities produced an ever-evolving foundation for me.

I benefitted from completing conventional instruments: reviewing issues and accomplishments; getting feedback from peers, subordinates, and bosses; making lists of skills and interests; and identifying my personality pattern. Having engaged in each of these assessment techniques, I'd come to know myself quite well—the good, the bad, and the ugly. And I found that I'd been my own worst critic. When I hear other women criticize themselves, I recognize the commonality of this trait in women.

Mindmapping

I created a "mindmap" of trunks and branches connecting everyone I knew (see next page): one major trunk for my last employer, another trunk for all previous employers, then branches for the managers, employees, customers, suppliers, advisers, investors, competitors, and industry groups. Each one created more branches, with their own employees and customers and with their families and communities.

I created a major trunk for each aspect of my life—my family, community, hobbies, and education. Prospects became yet another trunk, as I engaged with the employees, customers, suppliers, and advisers of prospective companies.

The mindmap included people I didn't know but would like to: authors of favorite books, leaders of admirable businesses, and consultants helping to create cultures where employees love to work. I discovered that I was meeting these very people by doing the things I loved to do.

What is a Mindmap?

A mindmap is a right-brain approach to outlining. Create a major branch for each major thought. Add minor branches for sub-sections, and branches off of those branches. Place only one word on each branch; that will open up new categories that you hadn't thought of the first time.

For example, one major part of your network may be your community. Within that are suppliers you personally use. Create a branch for dentist, doctor, hairdresser, mailman, child-care provider, and so forth. Then branching off from that, list the names of those you use. Each of them is a part of your network. And, of course, each of them have networks through their communities, education, customers, prior employers, and so forth.

Use bright colors. Draw pictures instead of words. Notice spaces and ask, "What belongs here?" Have fun. Post it on the wall. Live with it. See what else is to be added.

I Created My Vision

I could visualize the garden in full bloom, the rich textures, the vivid greens...

My vision is that men and women realize their choices in balancing family, self, career, and community without compromise.

This is my passion.

I live this vision, pulling the future into the present. Within the context of this vision, I was able to create my dream job description. With the help of coaches who could see me more clearly than I could see myself, it became obvious that I needed to match up needs with resources. In addition to the traditional location, compensation, and qualifications, my dream job description listed unusual items, such as:

- My responsibilities: using insight to reveal vision and needs
- My relationships: fun initiators
- My impact: contributing to the alignment of the corporate world with the needs of the earth
- My effort: being encouraged to take personal time for my family and myself

Attaining my dream job required strategizing: What are the steps between where I am now and where I want to be? I created a matrix that identified the characteristics of each stepping stone along the path of getting to what I wanted to be. I could bridge my corporate financial management to venture capital by being a CFO of a venture capital firm. For each interim step or position, I imagined what skills I'd develop, what impact I would make, and how I would be shaped. Seeing this as an evolutionary process made the "step job" feel like an integral part of the dream job.

The steps of the job search process overlapped. As I noticed openings with my name on them, I explored them. Naturally, the person at the other end of the conversation wanted to know

145

who I was. Three useful instruments evolved as I learned from and refined my vision and my presentation.

I designed one-minute, two-minute, and five-minute versions of my introduction, each covering my name, education, experience, outside interests, personal history, personal characteristics, and vision. I was happy to delve deeper into any one of these categories depending on the interest shown. I learned how important it was to trust my intuition in reinventing my introduction for each person I met.

Tending

I'd tilled, I'd fertilized, and I'd sown the seeds. Now I watered and nurtured my garden, in the beginning with only the faith that something was growing. Some plants turned out not to be what I wanted and had to be discarded, despite the care and love I'd given them. Some weeds threatened the lives of what I'd planted.

As I experienced how helpful people like to be, I came to discover how helpful I could be to others. In the course of conversation, I'd learn what they were up to and what they needed; often I had a lead or connection for them. Or one showed up the next day.

The lessons and opportunities were great during those last three months of increasing financial risk and uncertainty. I developed a faith in cosmic correlation between greater risk and greater return. Not only were better jobs showing up, but more of them were.

At this point, I realized that my sights had been focused on the Boston area for the past twelve years. What if I were to venture beyond my admittedly preferred geographical area and explore other possibilities? As my friend Jeanne advised, "Never turn down an offer before it's been extended." How wise. Why should I close off other opportunities in my search? My networking connected me with folks in Boulder, San Francisco, Lake Oswego, and Battle Creek. I got acquainted with regional and international organizations that were committed to the same global future that I wanted.

Logistically, I developed my own scale for evaluating all my opportunities. I rated each attribute of a prospective job on a scale of 1 to 5. The attributes included location as well as all the other qualities that I demanded in a new position. With 5 as the worst and 1 as the absolute best, I developed cumulative scores for each prospect. My "dream job" received a total of 1.5 when it found me.

Reaping

And then the garden started to blossom, one plant after another—and another. I would be tempted to pick one when another, more beautiful would appear. And then, finally, three exquisite plants bloomed at once. Picking one leaves the others no less valuable and beautiful.

Much of my career had been goal-driven, but what worked in my job search was to be the *target*. During the course of my search, I realized what really mattered to me. I described my dream job as one that is dynamic, diverse, empowering, financially rewarding, and win-win; that values resourcefulness, innovation, feminine-masculine balance, and learning.

I shared my list with everyone I met. "Will I find this in this industry? At this company?" I asked. "No, you won't" was information as useful as "Yes, you will." I loved seeing the passion for these values evoked in others who felt as I did; and I appreciated not spending my time on opportunities that did not fit.

Within two months of creating this list, a wonderful job showed up, as CFO of a values-driven venture capital firm. The people and the mission were everything I'd been looking for. But something wasn't right. I wasn't jumping at the opportunity. I looked for what was missing from my list and discovered that I'd neglected to include " fun," a quality missing from this professional firm.

"Fun" went on the list, and the next month a job showed up that, again, fulfilled my list. My financial resources were running out, the economy was lousy (implying poor job prospects), and still I found myself holding back. I couldn't put my finger on it until my friend Walter pointed out, "Jan, you are a leader. This company is not. You need to be with a leader." Bingo. He was absolutely right. I turned down the offer and added "leadership" to the list.

I was surprised when the job fulfilling all my expectations didn't show up the next month. I felt grateful for having learned the lessons from transition, and I felt ready for my next trapeze bar. What's missing from my list? I asked as I studied it one more time. Aha, I realized, I haven't listed "by when." I haven't said by when my dream job should show up. So I added to the list that my dream job should show up within a week and close within two weeks. The next two weeks were the most exhilarating and passionate time of my life. Three jobs showed up, each fulfilling my list. The hardest part of my career search was choosing among them.

> ### Criteria for My Dream Job
>
> DYNAMIC
> DIVERSE
> EMPOWERING
> FINANCIALLY REWARDING
> WIN-WIN
> RESOURCEFULNESS
> INNOVATION
> FEMININE-MASCULINE
>   BALANCE
> LEARNING
> FUN
> LEADERSHIP
> BY WHEN?

One never knows which seed will produce the dream job. Four months earlier, a ten-minute visit to an old college friend—one I hadn't seen in ten years—had revealed that his Big-6 accounting firm was receiving twenty-five unsolicited resumes a day in Boston alone. I figured mine was going nowhere—until I got a call. "Was I still available?" A fellow partner knew of an opening at a company being started by a friend in his church. Who would have guessed that that ten-minute visit would have led to the trapeze bar with my name on it?

I developed faith in the universe providing exactly what I'd asked for. When what showed up wasn't what I wanted, I looked back to see what was missing from my request. Having learned this lesson, having developed this faith, my lesson in *flying* was complete. I could grab on to and learn the lessons of the next trapeze bar with my name on it.

Continuum

This year's blooms may fade, but the soil is richer for their living; my spirit is undauntable in nurturing the roots for another season of growth.

A year and a half ago, I accepted a position as vice-president of finance with Loyalty Management Group, Inc., in Boston, a new company with prospects for rapid growth and a win-win idea. The founder's vision for lifetime customer relationships resonated for me. Our service promised that people could visit family and friends or just rest, relax, and recreate on vacation. Our impact would include people traveling places they'd never been, learning of and understanding cultures different from their own—a foundation for world harmony. This 6-employee company would grow to 150 during my tenure, providing a platform from which new ways of doing business could be developed, where employees loved to work and where all the stakeholders of the business—the customers, the suppliers, the investors, the employees, and the community—could seek and enjoy a synergistic win-win.

I'm still learning. I've learned that a dream job is not a destination; it's a part of my journey. It takes constant re-creating and a commitment to the processes, the values, and the "seasons" of growth.

I'll not forget what I learned: that the universe delivers what I ask of it. I will learn from what it delivers. I will ask for what I want.

I wish I knew and could thank whoever said:
Dare to be a Daniel
Dare to stand alone
Dare to have a purpose firm, and
Dare to make it known.

Anne Lippitt Rarich is director of management development and technical training for the business markets division of Liberty Mutual Insurance Group in Boston. She is also president of Learning Exchange. During her twenty-year career, she has been an instructor in entrepreneurship, marketing, and leadership; manager of human resource development in a division of Digital Equipment Corporation; a consultant to government and industry; and an elected official determining public education policy. She is a published author in the fields of career and management development as well as quality and the learning organization.

Rarich applies the principles of her consulting and training business in her leadership roles with various professional associations and community grass-roots initiatives. She has been the recipient of business excellence awards from *Working Woman* magazine and the Boston YWCA.

9

Organizational Renewal Through a Hunger for Meaning

Anne Lippitt Rarich

As a change agent working inside a large corporation for the past five years, I struggled with how one can positively affect a system that is operating as a dysfunctional organization.

One can feel victimized and powerless during times of indecision, inconsistent communication, and lack of direction in any organization. Although my past perspective comes from a Fortune 100 high-tech company, the symptoms are not unlike my experiences in other private and nonprofit organizations. The previous lack of leadership at the top has had a major impact on the roots of the organization as well as the general viability of the business. The lessons I learned working in a large system have been invaluable, and I realize that I have in fact been applying them in my community as an elected official and as an entrepreneur.

My experiences, knowledge, and conclusions have led me to believe that any successful transformation or renewal of an organization must begin with the individuals in that organization. Each individual must have his or her own sense of vision and direction before there can be a collective vision. There can be no sustainable organizationwide renewal without vision, an internal desire to change, and a collective shift in thinking and behavior.

Organizational Renewal

The world needs creative organizational leadership. Individuals are struggling to find meaning in and add value to the systems within which they live. My desire has been to pose a new approach to how we manage both ourselves and our organizations in these turbulent times. I do not see individual meaning as more important than the work that must be done by the leadership of an organization, but there needs to be equal emphasis on individuals becoming more self-directed and responsible rather than relying on or waiting for the dictates of others.

Organizational renewal is not a set of random acts. It will happen only if top policy makers are involved in the process, carefully planning for both change and a recycling of resources. In periods of rapid change, organizational leadership must creatively seek new directions, methods, approaches, and technologies.

Until recently, the prevailing paradigm has been that the CEO holds the key to any change and renewal within an organization. From my own experiences I conclude that this paradigm needs to shift. I believe that organizational renewal can occur only if there is a clear purpose and a self-reviewing process throughout the organization. Further, an openness is required for embracing the self-renewal process. Senior management needs to be open to reassessing intentions, vision, and new objectives, and individuals need to be open to learning how to learn.

Individuals who are continually clarifying and deepening their personal vision hold the key to a revitalized organization. The dilemma is how to create a culture that encourages this openness to change when everyone within the organization is adrift in ambiguity, uncertainty, and patterns of unpredictable competition.

My own work of personal transformation prepared me for new beginnings both within the corporate environment and beyond. I attempted to create a climate in which others who were seeking a renewal could attain it. I do not presume to have single-handedly caused an organizational change to begin, but I invite you to think about how one person's vision for potential breakthrough in a company, or any system, for that matter, might bring an organizational renewal effort into being. Like many multinational corporations facing exponential changes in technology and markets, the organization was in search of stability rather than looking for new innovations and approaches. Individuals who had been rewarded in the past for their creativity and courage were now at risk of losing their jobs.

The Corporate Experience

I joined a large Fortune 100 corporation in 1986 because I had been consulting with companies for many years and felt that my credibility as a consultant to organizations and systems would be enhanced by my walking in the shoes of those with whom I was consulting. It has been my belief and experience that to be most credible and effective in my work requires both an understanding of organizational principles and an in-depth knowledge and experience of how to apply them. These principles include strategic planning, productivity, standards, technical expertise, competitive responsiveness, and employee orientation. I grew up in an academic environment in which there was a lot of theorizing and modeling of other people's dilemmas and little firsthand application. Early in my career, I concluded that I had to experience and test potential applications before recommending or teaching them to others. Working inside the system would be a way of testing, improving, and challenging my theories.

I was initially hired to create, produce, and manage a training program for 450 middle managers in the United States.

This was a new initiative and would require a great deal of design as well as implementation skills and knowledge. The program was a remarkable success. My success was so noteworthy that I was promoted to a newly created position as human resource development manager.

In this role, I worked to educate both the human resource people and senior line management about the need for a "learning organization" culture. It was important to probe constantly and get consensus on what objectives and outcomes all parties were attempting to influence. Training had been viewed as a panacea but not an integral part of any business challenge or long-term investment in the employees. There had been little support for individuals applying new learning (outside the product development arena). We needed to create an environment in which employees who took an internal management course would immediately practice their newly acquired skills and be given support. A climate where learning is valued would ultimately lead to greater effectiveness of the individual, the group, and the company.

Through my efforts to align future business objectives and goals with management training courses, I was successful in establishing a corporate international management training program. Ultimately, a senior-level corporatewide board was developed to review future human resource curriculum investments to support and build future critical skills.

Markets began to change and sales started to decline. The need for transition strategies became critical. I was asked to work with a number of colleagues from different disciplines to orchestrate a response that would alleviate the need for layoffs. Everyone involved felt that we could really support the company and offer individuals a chance for profound growth and learning thus positioning the human resources with potential new strategies.

It was at this point that I became keenly aware of the disaster that was unfolding in the corporation. Not only were financial, service, and product strategies changing, but goals and targets were being missed because of changing markets, and there was no coordination in the system of roles and responsibilities. There was low employee tolerance for the changing business objectives and reorganizations. Employees were taking a disproportionate share of the blame for executive decisions and practices that were based on old responses to new challenges. There was no sense of "reciprocal responsibility"— that is, there was no sense of shared risk or reward—between management and workers for the development of new processes, whether for quality, cost containment, or concurrent engineering. The pain of a revitalization seems to fall most heavily on employees who have had the least responsibility for the organizational decline. Every week, employees were asked to implement new corporate initiatives that were not getting equal commitment from top management.

A survival climate existed when change needed to occur. Instead of creativity, courage, and opportunity, there was a sense of resignation, skepticism, aimlessness, alienation, and cowardice pervading the organization.

It was in this climate that I began to develop my own understanding of being personally influenced by a destructive external set of beliefs and attitudes. I wanted to be part of the solution—not to contribute to perpetuating the problem. I believed that the events that were unfolding provided an opportunity for constructive change, and I wanted to contribute. It took some major reflection, inquiry, and exploration on my part to realize that, at a personal level, I had lost touch with my core purpose and meaning.

My Personal Growth

I was caught up in the very culture that I wanted to change. I had to stop blaming others as well as myself for what was unfolding and ask what my unique purpose is. No one could do this work for me. No one else could articulate my purpose, values, and passion for me. I realized that if I was going to help anyone in the organization, I had better start with myself.

Where would I begin? How would I begin? What did I believe that I was accepting as a *truth*? What was I willing to let go of?

This process was akin to jumping into an abyss of "unknowing." I wanted to put off dealing with all the complexity of asking the right questions, of testing my resolve, and of articulating my deepest desires. I wanted to avoid coming up with the answers that must be put into action. The pain of stagnation, turf battles, and unclear direction were beginning to affect me emotionally and physically. I realized that my very existence was being tested. I was exhausted all the time. However, I knew that I had to follow my own heart and begin a journey for meaning, purpose, and commitment.

Once I began the journey, I realized that this could be a time of immense creativity and freedom. My normal resistance to ideas that meant change became an invitation to explore new possibilities. I started taking courses, reaching out to others who were open to change, and taking on tasks that would allow me to stretch and develop myself. One such activity was leading a task force to outline companywide standards for career development. It was during this process that I came to learn that it is the successful transitional work of the individual that can contribute to the renewal of both the individual and the organization.

There were times when I thought I was the only one struggling to get control and understand my spiritual anchors. I thought that others either were going through this process faster than I or did not care to engage in self-examination. Making an effort at reorientation is not easy and does require letting go of "the way we were."

I realized that everyone has their own timetable for this transition work, if they do it at all. I became impatient with myself and wanted to be done quickly with the discomfort of reprioritizing and sloughing off old ways of approaching my world. I wanted answers and did not even know what to ask. Personal fears and organizational wounds were not easy to let go of. I realized that this process might go on forever and that I would have to be satisfied with an endless journey of discovery.

At first, there was nothing I could connect to. I decided that what I was being offered was a clean slate. Slowly, I came to reconnect to my core purpose and the values that came out of this purpose. It was choosing what "felt right" rather than what I "thought." It was the feeling of being reconnected to myself, not to an organization or a single set of work demands. It was knowing that I had to make this journey alone, but not unsupported. Others were sharing their stories with me, and we began to support each other.

I saw how my purpose was different from anyone else's and in conflict with that of the corporation. This misalignment was the source of my "dis-ease" and left me with a sense of being drained. I remembered what I had wanted to accomplish when I was a teenager and thought about what I wanted to do in the future—before I died. This helped me to realize that my purpose really had not changed—just the *context* had. As I became clearer about my purpose and passion, I found myself gaining confidence, self-disclosing with trusted allies, establishing a vision of new possibilities and renewed energy to persevere with those who were not feeling either courageous or visionary.

The Creation of the Knowledge Networking Forum

One of the cultural norms that were supported by most organizations in the corporation was the practice of "core groups," which were set up as a means for people with similar problems to support one another. These were self-managed "pods" of employees who would meet to support one another around a core issue. Many of these groups were made up solely of women, who found safety in these core groups to explore their concerns. A number of the groups decided that it would be helpful to network on common themes, so each group came to a steering committee meeting every other month to discuss issues and report on pet projects being done on an individual's own time.

The chaos in the organization was affecting the quality of the work that was being produced. People were no longer feeling safe to speak their minds, let alone try new ideas or question old ones. It was a time of great ambiguity and mistrust. It was time to be creative and take action. As facilitator of the steering committee, I proposed that we create a forum to which anyone in the company could come. The purpose would be to share companywide resources in one location, to celebrate women's contributions, and to present future business directions that the company was in the midst of adopting and implementing. I agreed to take lead responsibility for the implementation of this forum. No one else was in a place to take the risk. I had a newfound sense of how my purpose needed to be made manifest and saw this as a challenge. I wanted the opportunity to showcase possibilities rather than dilemmas.

I recruited people and resources from all levels of the organization to get help. I obtained the free use of a closed-down manufacturing site. The manufacturing floor would be retrofitted to facilitate a possible group of 225 people.

Within twelve hours of sending out an invitation on the corporate E-mail network to over 300 people, mostly women who were current members of support groups, we had 75 people signed up. By the time the event was held, there were 250 attendees and 450 on a waiting list for the one-day forum.

The Knowledge Networking Forum was a successful event. Formal feedback told us that the most important things learned by participants included:

"Women's uniqueness can have a positive impact on business."

"Resources were great and were reminders of collective power."

"I now have a better understanding of [the company's] direction through presentations and know I can play a role."

The commitments that were made by participants at this event included:

"I will take time to develop a network."

"I will share copies of handouts with others on my team—especially share information on continuous learning concepts and collaboration."

"I will be more open about sharing my own personal commitment to excellence."

As a result of this event, there were many requests for my support in establishing other networks and forums within the organization. Managers who had been too busy with shifting organizational demands were hearing how a day of resource sharing and business communication was giving a renewed sense of organizational direction to employees. Employees now had knowledge of choices within the corporation. They could finally appreciate that the corporation had provided some reciprocal resources for learning.

Personal Mastery, Key to a Learning Organization

For renewal to occur in an individual, an organization, or a community, the decision to change and the actions that result in renewal must occur inside each individual. No decree or management initiative alone can force a change to begin. The environment may influence an individual's desire to examine his or her values, beliefs, and norms, but it cannot dictate what the specifics of an individual's change in outlook will be.

This is a most critical area and referred to by Peter Senge (1990) in his book *The Fifth Discipline* as "personal mastery."

Personal mastery is the discipline of continually clarifying and deepening our personal vision, of focusing our energies, of developing patience and of seeing reality objectively.

A Great Learning Must Occur

No one event is going to change the environment of a corporation. If real learning is to take place, there must be a continual examination of interrelationships among employee readiness, market realities, competitive products, and economic conditions. I am convinced that all parts of the organization must come together in a new pattern of operation, roughly at the same time. This is termed a *collective mind shift* or *mind-set change*. At my Fortune 100 corporation, great excitement and belief in new possibilities have come with a recent change in leadership. It is a systemwide mind-set that is looking at future possibilities rather than staying stuck in the past. It is the new promise as I write this essay. There is a new sense of accountability, competence, and being valued. The response to customer needs has more importance and has led to early predictions of potential renewal.

The Survivors

Currently, downsizing is taking place within the company. There has been little attention paid to the people who have remained in the company. Although I was laid off, I have been working with colleagues through the company's quality organization to establish a revitalization effort for survivors. As an external consultant, I have a unique perspective in working with this company. This effort has been successfully launched by the introduction of a course entitled Rediscovering the Passion at Work.

To initiate the course, the employee involvement group in the quality program office issued an invitation to all middle managers asking them to indicate their interest in participating. Potential participants were screened to make sure they would get maximum benefit from the course. If people were in the midst of personal crisis, we recommended that they get more specialized help.

The course is four days in length, with a two-week break before the final session. At the end of the first three days, feelings have been expressed, and participants feel safe. Each participant has articulated to the other attendees his or her purpose. Participants are encouraged to identify one action that they will put into practice within their work group during the next two weeks that springs from their purpose. When everyone returns for the final day, they share their experiences and learning. Many find that they now approach work differently; others are surprised at the consequences. Whatever the outcome of the action, there is an opportunity for learning and a beginning of the renewal process.

A steering committee of graduates has been set up to monitor and initiate other activities that will promote the renewal effort. If employees wish to be competitive in the information age, it is important to learn new ideas, concepts, and realities to replace outmoded skills, knowledge, and attitudes.

The process of self-examination has led me on a path of action that requires conviction, courage, leadership, risk taking, and constant support from a core group of trusted colleagues. I have continued the search for meaning and have learned the importance of community and relationships. Without the support of other "works in progress," this transition would have been impossible to navigate. The ability to provide a healing atmosphere for one another has been critical.

Individuals are always struggling for compatibility or alignment between organizational direction and personal growth. There is a yearning, too, for meaningful work. Most modern business history has been characterized by patterns of management dictating the direction of the organization to its employees. We live in a time of complex systems that call for a new paradigm. When individual purpose is aligned with the culture and directions of the organization, responsibility for the whole organization and maximum effectiveness will be achieved.

As a change agent, I have been privileged to influence many aspects of different organizational renewal efforts. It has been my personal mission to *be* the change or the renewal that I seek for an organization and for the world. Our hearts direct both the chaos and the renewal in our companies and the world. The hope and the challenge are in each of us. Collaboration, understanding, courage, and love are needed to survive in the renewal that I want for myself and the world.

161

Anne Rarich had the quotation below pinned on
her office wall for inspiration.

The Way of Transformation

The man who, being really on the Way, falls upon hard times in the world will not, as a consequence, turn to that friend who offers him refuge and comfort and encourages his old self to survive. Rather, he will seek out someone who will faithfully and inexorably help him to risk himself, so that he may endure the suffering and pass courageously through it, thus making of it a "raft that leads to the far shore." Only to the extent that man exposes himself over and over again to annihilation, can that which is indestructible arise within him. In this lies the dignity of daring. Thus, the aim of practice is not to develop an attitude which allows a man to acquire a state of harmony and peace wherein nothing can ever trouble him. On the contrary, practice should teach him to let himself be assaulted, perturbed, moved, insulted, broken and battered—that is to say, it should enable him to dare to let go his futile hankering after harmony, surcease from pain, and a comfortable life in order that he may discover, in doing battle with the forces that oppose him, that which awaits him beyond the world of opposites. The first necessity is that we should have the courage to face life, and to encounter all that is most perilous in the world. When this is possible, meditation itself becomes the means by which we accept and welcome the demons which arise from the unconscious—a process very different from the practice of concentration on some object as a protection against such forces. Only if we venture repeatedly through zones of annihilation can our contact with Divine Being, which is beyond annihilation, become firm and stable. The more a man learns wholeheartedly to confront the world that threatens him with isolation, the more are the depths of the Ground of Being revealed and the possibilities of new life and Becoming opened.

From *The Way of Transformation* by Karlfried Graf Durckheim (Unwin Hyman, LTD. London, 1980)

Jeanne Borei is an educator and futurist with an academic background in philosophy, public relations, and the performing arts. She is an active member of various organizations concerned with global community consciousness, including the World Business Academy, from which she received the 1991 Willis Harman Award.

She is presently the director of human resources for the Tel-A-Train Corporation, an international organization based in Chattanooga, Tennessee, where she has been instrumental in the company's taking steps toward a shift in philosophy and culture that is clearly paving the way for the direction of business in the future. As a pioneer in this effort, Tel-A-Train is one of the first U.S. private companies to commit themselves to a total community-building process.

The chapter was adapted from an article by Ms. Borei in *World Business Academy Perspectives* (Vol 6 No 2 – 1992).

10

Chaos to Community: One Company's Journey Toward Transformation

Jeanne Borei

Over the past 60 years, just as we've developed a technology that we can use to blow ourselves off the face of the earth, we've also very quietly and unknown to most people developed a technology we can use to make peace.... I call it community-building.

M. Scott Peck, M.D.

"No one said this was going to be easy. Warm fuzzies are not guaranteed. Authentic communication, honesty, this is the best we can promise—assuming you reach community. And that, my friend, is not a guarantee." This was the message I received just before we headed down a road toward transformation. Not an easy message—certainly not one to invoke security or self-assuredness, especially when one's "life" is on the line. In this case, it was the life of our company.

Some History

In July of 1973, my father, Perry Lane, an engineer and visionary, saw a need arising in industry and education for effective, quality technical and safety training. Combining energy, creativity, and limited finances, he set out to establish the company that has now become a leader in a worldwide arena.

Over the years, various family members have been involved in the company's management. This factor inadvertently gave birth to a spirit of "family" that has permeated the attitude of daily operations, affecting, in varying degrees, the personal lives of many of our employees. This really hit home for me when two of our employees chose to get married in our company conference room, with company personnel and the local NBC-TV affiliate in attendance.

In a word, for better or worse, we had become "home" for a substantial number of employees. This same sense of belonging and caring became the foundation for the way in which we deal with our customers. Our reputation for excellent service and quality of product grew rapidly, allowing us to enjoy a genuine rich taste of success and reward.

What, then, caused us to question that something might be wrong—that our very survival might be at stake?

It was not any one occurrence or circumstance. It was, rather, an accumulation of day-to-day, year-to-year experiences that one by one added to a steady, slow buildup of pressure. We were headed toward an inevitable day of reckoning. We didn't know it until it was on top of us. This state, what I would eventually come to recognize as "chaos," was not noticed earlier because of the daily successes we experienced with our customers and each other.

The first signs, and the most obvious, were seen in the financial reports. Less obvious, in the beginning, was that the "family" began experiencing discord through interdepartmental conflict and miscommunications, misunderstanding between home and outside offices, an increase in individual mistrust and confrontation, development of subcultures, and enhancement of codependent relationships in several layers of the company.

One of the most glaring signs of discontent surfaced in our decision-making process. As time went on, more and more decisions came as a result of frustration or desperation. Two scenarios were common. In one, innumerable meetings would be held before a decision was made. There was always a need for "further discussion," so that the result would be either no decision or crisis decision making. In the other scenario, decisions were arrived at by one or two managers, who should have involved other players in the process but found that too cumbersome. This latter scenario was a serious cause of miscommunication and ill will.

Recognizing a Need for Change

Recently, I heard someone say that a person (or organization) will ask for help when the pain gets bad enough. Bit by bit, incident by incident, the pain in our organization was increasing. We continued to have our moments in the sun, those times when all seemed okay, but something was beginning to surface, an unidentified feeling that let us know that everything was not as it should be. I can look back now and see that though we were not aware of it, we were operating as a dysfunctional family. The daily routine of operating from what I now understand to be crisis or chaos mode was what we assumed to be "normal." It's no wonder we did not foresee and certainly were not prepared for the state in which we began to find ourselves.

To be honest, I am not sure what we could or would have done differently over the years. I do know that at each stage of growth, we did the best we knew how at any given time. We had attracted some of the most loyal and hardworking employees any company could hope for. A philosophical observer might say that we had to go through what we did to get to where we are. All I know is that where we were is not where we wanted to be. Change was inevitable.

167

Rarely does change come without chaos and confusion. I get encouragement from James Gleick's words in his book *Chaos* (1987):

Chaos is a science of process rather than a state, of becoming rather than being.

I had to believe that our chaos was not permanent, however long it had been with us, and that with effort and commitment, we could redirect our energies toward order of a better kind.

Our move toward community actually began with a World Business Academy retreat in May of 1991, when I participated in my first community-building workshop based on the design described in M. Scott Peck's *The Different Drum* (1987). It was here that I first discovered a way of being that astounded me— a way in which people, whether two or many, whether or not they knew each other, could be authentic and honest with each other and could, from this place of authenticity, reach true consensus and deal with task-oriented issues in a truly productive and effective manner.

I was so moved by this three-day experience that immediately upon my return home, I shared it with the president of our company. I was convinced that what I had just witnessed in the retreat could offer hope for our organization. Little did I know the impact that my sharing would have. I was not aware at the time that on the day I left for the retreat, a meeting had been called with our remaining managers to discuss the state of the company. The timing was perfect.

In early June of 1991, I was asked to contact Ann Hoewing and Ed Groody, the two consultants who had facilitated the Academy's community-building workshop. We wanted them to facilitate the same workshop for our fourteen managers. The tide was about to turn.

We gathered in early September at Guntersville State Park in Alabama. The stage was set. I remember the comment our president made: "There's no going back now. I'm committed."

It was not magic. It was not fantasy. It was real! It was genuine! And what was truly surprising was that the process itself is a gentle one. The results, however, may be anything but gentle. They may even be life-changing! What is certain is that whatever the result, it would be real and authentic.

The Process

The process began with Ann and Ed explaining guidelines for building "community." Scott Peck's definition of community is "a group of two or more people who, regardless of the diversity of their backgrounds (social, spiritual, educational, ethnic, economic, political, etc.) have been able to accept and transcend their differences, enabling them to communicate effectively and openly and work together toward goals identified as being for their common good."

The guidelines include the use of "I statements" wherever possible, instead of "we statements" that assume and generalize; being aware of excluding others or self; and speaking when moved to speak (and not speaking when not moved to speak). One guideline, which probably would not be used outside the formal community circle, was particularly helpful, though awkward to get used to. This was starting statements with "My name is…" each time we wished to speak. This not only created an immediate space for someone to speak but forced us to "own" what we said. It compelled me, for instance, to really think before I spoke and helped to create a space for any feeling I might be having.

Feeling is a key word in community. As we began to move through the process, it became clear that getting in touch and staying in touch with feelings was crucial. Feelings, I learned, are a great barometer for letting us know whether we are coming from a place of authenticity.

In our workshop we learned that there are four steps to reaching "community."

Four Steps to Community

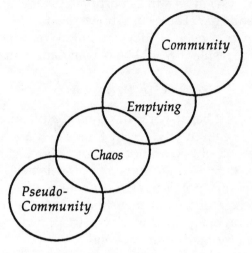

Groups generally move through the four steps in the order depicted in the diagram, beginning with the first circle, Pseudo-Team or Pseudo-Community, and progressing upward through the stages of Chaos and Emptying toward the top circle Community or Authentic Team. Whether or not this final stage is reached depends entirely on the dynamics and commitment of the group. It is important to note that no group stays in Community *all the time*. The tendency is to move in and out of the stages. What is important is to recognize where you are in the diagram.

Pseudo-Community can be recognized when those in a group are coming from a place of what I call "plastic" or superficial concern (similar to a cocktail party environment), where everyone is "nice" and each person assumes that "we're all alike," "we don't have any problems," and "we all get along."

In the community building process, Pseudo-Community goes into Chaos when differences begin to arise—individuals in the group begin to realize that they may not be the same as the others. Diversity begins to show its face, and Chaos sets in. This is usually apparent when a person is sharing a thought, and the group responds by quickly jumping in with other ideas and thoughts rather than truly hearing what that person has to say.

170

When no one is really listening to anyone else, conflict, confusion, and frustration result. Chaos is not inherently either bad or good—it is simply a stage to be recognized, especially when decisions have to be made. Many companies never get beyond the stage of Chaos, and, unfortunately, this is the stage in which they often make decisions. This leads to crisis management—definitely home territory for our company.

If I have learned anything from this process, it's that you do not, repeat, do not make decisions when in Chaos mode. So how do you get beyond this to a place where effective and enduring decisions can be made? The key lies in the next stage, that of Emptying—a point at which most companies and many individuals never arrive.

In Emptying, a person begins to look at him- or herself rather than at the group. It is here that old baggage may be discarded, that obstacles that have blocked personal communication and caused misunderstandings will begin to appear and to be shed. This is often a very emotional time for groups, as it is during this stage that walls come down, facades are exposed, and truth begins to show its face. In Guntersville, my own experience of Emptying was life-changing. I found myself sharing hurts and angers toward one of the managers in the group that I had held inside for more than ten years. I realized that the only way I could get beyond this (hopefully to be a better person, as well as a better manager) was to lance open the wound and allow the infection to drain out. It was not easy, but it was necessary for genuine healing to take place. The key element was the group. Somehow, the group's energy had made it safe enough for this interaction to occur. This was very different from any group interaction that I had ever before experienced, certainly in a business setting. Others in the group raised and addressed their own issues within the safe space that we as a group had unknowingly, almost mysteriously created.

We spent two days walking through Pseudo-Community, Chaos, and Emptying—a sequence that was predictable but not ensured and was created by the dynamic of the group itself, with near-silent skillful facilitation from Ann and Ed. At the end of that time, we somehow found ourselves in a state of being unlike any that I have ever known before in the work environment. We were *in* Community!

How did we know? For me, it was an inner feeling, a knowing that communication with each other was different—very different. I found myself, as did others in the group, speaking from a place of "I" rather than "we" or "they." Outwardly, there seemed to be more focus, a new ability to deal with tasks efficiently and productively. The lack of suspicion of hidden agendas and a genuine desire to reach consensus on solutions to problems were taking root. The baggage and obstacles of all the previous years were beginning to be addressed and, in many cases, removed. As a group, we began to feel a hope and to experience a healing that I would not have thought possible prior to this experience.

Back to Work

"Okay, what happens Monday, when we all return to the workplace?" A legitimate question, as we each voiced concern about how *real* this experience was in the light of everyday reality. Would it, could it, really make a difference?

The results were immediate. One by one, employees began making comments about how different we were. On the whole, it seemed that, as a management team and as individuals, we were more patient, more willing to listen, genuinely wanting our employees' opinions and involvement. There was no doubt that something significant had occurred in Guntersville. There was no going back to the way we had been. As a management group, we were committed to moving forward, using the community-building process as the vehicle to take us there.

When we returned from our retreat, even though much had begun to change (particularly attitudes), it was evident that we still had a long way to go. We were not sure what the next steps should be. It was not until late December, several months after the retreat, that we were forced to face this question. Experiencing a familiar sense of building frustration, we were determined not to lose the spirit that we had created on that extraordinary September weekend, falling back into old "business as usual" patterns. We found it necessary to design tools or gauges to monitor our own health. Although our first attempt was arrived at more by default than by design, it was one of the best steps that we could have taken to keep us on the path we had chosen. We decided to commit every other Friday morning to "community circle" meetings, in which we would implement the formalized process that we had experienced at Guntersville. This was quite a step for us. Friday mornings were our traditional time for management meetings to review weekly reports and deal with other company matters. This step was not necessarily meant to be a permanent one, but it would be a beginning toward monitoring our road to health.

As a management team, we also committed ourselves to what has been the most crucial step yet—taking all of our U.S. employees through the community-building process. Our president was determined that we all "sing out of the same hymn book." If, as a collective, we are coming from this place of "community," particularly when decisions are being made, any problems that we as a company have had in the past or might face in the future have a real chance of being solved. In May of 1992, under the skillful guidance of Ann and Ed, we took the last of our employees through the process.

The part of the process that involved the managers and the changes that occurred from September 1991 to the spring of 1992 we have designated as Phase One. It was during this period that I saw our management group begin to learn how to truly work together as an effective work team and to come together in agreement on the importance of continuing the process of community-building in the middle of task-oriented projects, as well as everyday meetings and interactions.

Phase Two began when we started taking the rest of our employees, in groups of no more than twenty-five employees each, through community-building. This was done department by department, including outside offices.

The immediate result was a welcome one. We each seemed to be viewing each other differently. Except for a few who were still working through the Emptying stage, individuals were becoming less fearful of being truthful and straightforward in meetings and personal interactions. Hierarchical intimidations, warranted or not, seemed to have lessened considerably. For example, employees who previously might have been afraid to voice feelings and opinions to management have become more willing to share what is on their minds.

How all this has affected the proverbial bottom line, at the time of this writing, is in part still to be seen. I can say that morale in our workplace has made a 180-degree turn. Age-old problems of productivity, lack of an effective decision-making process, ineffective or unstated company policies, and interpersonal and interdepartmental conflict are now being addressed and either have been resolved or are in the process of being resolved.

I am clearly aware that we have a long way to go in some areas, but I am convinced that the healing has begun. I would like to think that what we have done might give other companies the courage to take similar risks—that our journey toward transformation might shed light on a path that is leading toward transformation of business on a global scale, and that we, in some way, are helping to create what I believe may be the *new paradigm* in business.

Hope Xaviermineo is a free-lance writer living in northern California. In her senior year of college, Hope was paralyzed in an auto accident. The next six years were spent in and out of the hospital. Using visualizations, experimental surgery, and other alternative methods, she recovered her ability to walk again. In 1983, Hope moved from Washington, D.C. to San Francisco and spent the next five years learning how to rejoin and participate in the world.

For two years she owned a management consulting company. It was there that she began writing about the changing role of business. She is currently working on a book about her accident and subsequent recovery.

11

A World We've Only Dreamed Of

Hope Xaviermineo

A powerful vision can create miracles. Many of us have read this, some of us believe it, and a few of us have the deep personal experience of bringing an *impossibility* into a reality through a complete commitment to a personal vision. I am one of those people.

At the tender age of twenty-one, still full of youthful exuberance and enjoying my college year in 1977, I was hit with a major tragedy. A drunk truck driver plowed into the rear end of a car in which I was a passenger, leaving me paralyzed from the waist down. I was told I would never walk again and spent the next six years in bed.

After I acknowledged my new status in life, I became determined to walk again. Not one doctor gave me any encouragement. People believed that I was delusional. But I developed a vision that was so powerful that I could not even imagine *not* walking!

By the time I reached twenty-seven, I had endured a variety of surgeries and a cadre of physicians and surgeons. But after six years of inner and outer work, I could walk again!

If you saw me today, you'd never know that I once had a physical malady. I'm a vital, active woman with no visible evidence of the accident. I am still surprised that my body was once pronounced permanently disabled.

How Did I Do the Impossible?

How did this miracle happen? How was I able to achieve a result that no one believed I could accomplish? It began with a vision. I had a deep, personal commitment to a very clear and powerful vision. This "miracle" began inside me—with a belief that I could recover my ability to walk.

After my own vision was clear, I made a commitment to see it through, with passion, determination, and intention. This commitment and intention allowed me to remain determined even when it seemed obvious that I was attempting to accomplish the impossible. I recall a favorite writing:

> *Until one is committed there is hesitancy, the chance to draw back, always ineffectiveness. Concerning all acts of initiative (and creation), there is one elementary truth, the ignorance of which kills countless ideas and splendid plans: that the moment one definitely commits oneself, then providence moves too. All sorts of things occur to help one that would never otherwise have occurred. A whole stream of events issues from the decision, raising in one's favor all manner of unforeseen incidents and meetings and material assistance, which no man could have dreamt would have come his way. I have learned a deep respect for one of Goethe's couplets: "Whatever you can do, or dream you can, begin it. Boldness has genius, power, and magic in it."*

—W. H. Murray,
The Scottish Himalayan Expedition
(J. M. Dent and Sons, 1951)

178

While I was committed to walking again I did have a number of setbacks. One particular surgery, I recall, was a disaster—making me worse instead of better. At one point, I was even accused of malingering by my physicians, quite possibly because they were so frustrated that their attempts were not producing progress.

Thanks to the clarity I possessed—the clarity that comes only when you have that kind of commitment and vision—my determination and drive *increased* with these setbacks. I kept telling myself, "The process will evolve."

How I Became an Observer

One of the benefits of being confined to bed for six years was that I was able to watch the world from a unique position. All my basic needs were being addressed, yet I was not a normal participant in the world. I didn't go to a job each day or travel around town or go shopping. I chose to eliminate television from my life. I began reading—probably three or four newspapers each day along with fifteen or so magazines a month.

I watched the world through the eyes of someone who was quite detached—just a pure observer of it all. It was after I immersed myself in this "global observation" that I began to realize the degree to which human beings unnecessarily endure pain or abuse.

It occurred to me that there has to be a better way—that human beings have a higher purpose than to abuse each other and themselves while they are alive. It is in the spirit of this reflection that I envision a future for humankind that may seem just as "impossible" as my being able to walk again.

I ask myself, "Why not apply this same passion, this same level of commitment, to creating a positive future for all human beings, living in harmony as a true community of diverse people?"

Where do we start? As you may already have realized, we start with ourselves—each and every one of us.

Which institutions have the greatest potential for changing us? In my view, they are our educational system and the business community. Since this is a business book, I'll focus on the potential role of business in helping us into a new reality. So, let's examine ourselves and the institution of business.

The Way It Is—Abusive and Separate

Imagine describing the color green to someone who has never seen or been exposed to anything remotely resembling green. How would you explain what you see in such a way that they could also envision the color green? It would take great care and patience—with an open mind and heart—on the part of both the teacher and the student. It is with similar care and patience that I ask that you read this essay.

Our world is experiencing upheaval and drastic change. Some call this a transformation—a death of the old ways of behaving and believing, and the birth of a new way not yet totally revealed. New possibilities for business will come out of the new realities we create for ourselves. Throughout this creative process, we are learning how to prosper and grow by gaining greater awareness and increased consciousness. We are just beginning to understand that we can live in a different way, with a new perspective of harmony and balance, traveling a more peaceful path to the future.

The business community, like each individual, is a part of this incredible transformation. What could change, and what are the new possibilities for business? The answers can be found as much within each one of us as they can inside each company.

Many people report that when they take a closer look at their lives and at the world around them—with objectivity and without judgment—they feel sad, let down, discouraged, disappointed. Some feel outraged. Still others feel hopeless and petrified. Most of us have developed a gross intolerance for anything that we don't *know* and understand. We have lived by our limitations, rather than our ability to expand and see beyond. We find it difficult to see others and accept their varied skin colors, unique religious choices, different social and personal values, and diversity of financial status. Nations, governments, companies, and individuals have been consciously and unconsciously, covertly and overtly, splitting apart in the perceived need for "self-preservation"—in the name of holding on to what they believe is right. With each generation, harsher divisions and wider gaps have been separating us from each other in our effort to protect our children, our nations, our governments, our environment, our companies, and ourselves.

This lack of understanding and minimal acceptance of most of our world has contributed to our judging each other and becoming addicted to what we possess. In turn, our addictions—whether life threatening or a mild distraction, conscious or unconscious—allow us to tolerate inhumanities that would otherwise turn our stomachs. When we take an honest look at these inhumanities—those self-imposed and those we accept from outside of ourselves—we can see that they are obviously abusive.

Whether we abuse ourselves or tolerate the abuse that everyday life throws at us, we are left empty and cold, sometimes angry—always with low self-esteem. When we've been abused enough, we lose our sense of dignity and self-worth.

We tend to associate abuse with physical, emotional, or sexual violation, but it can exist in different forms and intensities. Businesses are abused by employees who lie about being sick in order to take days off. They are abused by union rules and government laws that allow people to keep their jobs without performing with impeccability or integrity. We abuse our bodies, our environment, and our spirits. The quality of our lives diminishes in direct proportion to the amount of abuse we experience.

A Rude Awakening

Within a few months of beginning a new job in 1984, I had a rude awakening. I discovered that a significant number of people wake up each day, leave their homes, and do things they'd rather not be doing. I'd hear statements like "At least I don't have to work for anyone else," "Luckily, I don't have to work too many hours so I can do what I really want to do," "At least I don't have to take it home with me," "It pays the bills," and "At least it's a job." Many of us have grown accustomed to hearing these phrases and experiencing the energy behind them. We either laugh them off or brush them aside with a tacit agreement or gesture. If someone had this attitude about any other part of their life, we would bluntly say to them, "Why are you doing it, then?"

Work is commonly accepted as a negative and "necessary evil" in our lives. This same unhappiness and resignation are present in the personal part of many people's lives as well. This isn't true for everyone, of course, but there is an abundance of unhappiness being tolerated, from migrant workers to corporate executives. How can anyone—business or person—truly prosper in this environment?

Spending most of your time doing something you don't like is abusive. Since World War II, companies have been consistently asking employees to "work harder" by putting in more time, more energy, and more effort—sometimes for less money. Many businesses are offering less value and charging their customers more. If we all focused less on the dollar and what it buys, the business world and individuals would see new possibilities and reasons to "work" together that we can't even fathom now.

We do a lot in the name of self-preservation—as a planet, as nations, as groups, and as individuals. We have developed a way of living our lives as if we were separate from any larger whole. We have segregated ourselves in the name of survival; yet the truth is that we are all a part of a much greater whole. We are synergistic in every way. Our whole is greater than the sum of our parts, yet we keep splitting apart, "bettering" ourselves at another's expense. Fear is at the root of our facing off with one another. We are afraid of losing what we have rather than taking a risk for something unknown. Like generations before us, and the children we teach now, we have been conditioned to compete out of fear. If you win, I lose. Therefore, I must win, and you must lose.

Most people treat their work or business life as separate from the rest of their life. We cannot expect business to shift and support the transitions each of us is going through if we hold ourselves as "separate." It is impossible to support or be supported by what we are separate from.

Breakdown

Are most businesses prospering now? Is our world prospering now? What will a successful business look like in the twenty-first century? What will an alive, prospering, and thriving individual look like in the twenty-first century? The answers to these questions are directly related to one another.

We are in a *breakdown* of our world as we have come to know it. What we've inherited and what we've created no longer work. How can we be sure? New possibilities are "discussed" and plans are "implemented," but the magnitude of homelessness, war, debt, crime, violence, hunger, low self-esteem, lack of integrity, corruption, stress, and disease has become so overwhelming that people are feeling reluctant acceptance and mass resignation.

Look around at what you believe isn't working or what needs to change. Did these situations exist ten, twenty, or thirty years ago? If so, imagine how you felt about these circumstances then. Notice how you feel now. The very things that convince us that our world isn't working are on the rise in out-of-control proportions.

We consume and we go into debt. The result is economic chaos and imbalance. Nations, businesses, and individuals are spending more money than they have. The economy is leaning toward collapse. This fiscal irresponsibility is leading to the breakdown of our world. Our level of consumption is one of the biggest contributors to the destruction of our environment. We are showing signs of easing up on consumption, but we are still holding on to our "old" way of conducting our lives and our businesses. Third World countries and the former Eastern bloc nations still want to be like the West—to consume and borrow. They believe, as we did, that these actions will get rid of the problems they are facing.

Businesses and individuals are looking for answers—new ways of relating to one another. Most are looking for *external* solutions, even though, by now, it should be obvious that pointing fingers and blaming "them" for our condition gains us little. When each of us takes care of our own spirit, our own thoughts and actions, we can begin to create and work together in true partnership, without separateness. This leads us to a sense of community.

Creating Community

The dictionary defines *community* as "a unified body of people." We are entering a time when it is *crucial* to live as a unified body of individuals, as a *global community*. Community is shaped by the way we relate to one another and ourselves according to cultural and spiritual guidelines. Community is first an attitude, a state of heart and mind; then it is a form, or structure. It is an authentic partnership between and among humans and all other forms of life. Separateness and community are mutually exclusive.

But how do we get there? We get there by assuming 100 percent responsibility for our own lives and the role each of us plays, whether we are a business or an individual. It is important to realize that we are talking about drastic changes, not restructuring what already exists. After all, that's what a transformation is. We are in a period when we are changing the very essence of our existence. Business is facing the same changes individuals are—changing the very essence of its existence. By becoming a part of the creation of a true community, the business world will be creating new possibilities for its role in the lives of everyone.

Because most working people spend a large percentage of their waking hours "at work," and nearly everyone interacts with business as a customer of some sort, business is a major catalyst for change. The logistical details of community will develop when individuals and businesses commit themselves to creating the *spirit* of community together.

The new role for business will extend beyond merely providing jobs and work. The main objective of business will no longer be only the generation of profits; its objectives will be expanded to include enhancing and enriching the lives of each individual associated with the enterprise. Companies will provide environments where work fosters personal growth rather than distracting from it. Our jobs will become a *part* of our total life, rather than *dominating* it.

People's priorities are changing. Healthy relationships are replacing external self-gratification as a primary aspiration. There is public pressure for more time with family and friends and for quality time with oneself. People want to live from the same level of integrity in both their personal and professional lives—to have balance in their lives.

As the co-creator of community, the business world can serve itself and all of us. A deep connection can be woven among business, individuals, and our world, bringing them all together as one unified body.

Corporate Realities

How would companies plan for their changing role in our lives? A good rule of thumb: Whatever used to be your way of conducting business will probably change. Be open to altering and testing the waters *everywhere*—the way research is done; what is researched; ways of interacting with your employees, customers, stockholders, other businesses, government. Changes will include what and how policy is determined, how decisions are made, pay structures, vacations, work hours, what product is produced, what service is rendered, how customers are charged, how customers can pay—the list is endless.

We will still be concerned with money and profit and loss. That is the present reality. It cannot and should not be ignored. The best way to be a part of any transition is to participate in *exactly* what we want to change. While business is concerned with the bottom line today, it can be creating tomorrow by educating itself, its employees, shareholders, and customers, and other businesses. Education is gaining knowledge through a process. Tremendous numbers of people are touched by the business world, and the business community is the most powerful body of people on the planet. For this reason, it is our greatest resource for effecting positive change and creating community. An alliance between business and people committed to gaining knowledge about what's next for all of us can create miracles.

The structure and format of the discovery process are less important than the content and context of the process. Intention determines the content. Fearlessness, truth, and trust determine the context. We must be willing to ask the questions not yet asked. We must be willing to sit without answers and solutions. We are talking about creating an entirely new way of relating to ourselves, to one another, and to our planet—an entirely new role for business. As Albert Einstein stated, "The world will not evolve past its current state of crisis by using the same thinking that created the situation."

As business and people become a community, business will become a part of the whole person, and the whole person will be able to become a part of the business with which it is associated. Imagine if we brought 100 percent of ourselves to work every day! Being fully present at work could result in miracles—at our desks, in our meetings, behind counters, at computers, on the assembly line, under cars—everywhere people work.

Individuals in the business world, working together to create community, can reduce the pain and chaos we are witnessing and feeling as we change. A new and vital role for business can be created in our lives.

When business supports employees' growth, new visions can be created for a positive, sustainable future. There are as many possible visions as there are people to create them.

A New Vision

The following is *my* vision for how people, organizations, and society might interact in the future:

- *The business environment is a place where people play, learn, and work together in the deepest and purest sense.*

- *Everyone works, likes it, and wants to work because their experience on the job adds to their growth and is a vital part of their entire life.*

- *There are leaders without hierarchy.*

- *Business recognizes that our physical health is part of our mental and spiritual health. Business provides opportunities for* all *forms of health care.*

- *It no longer occurs to any business to lie or cheat. Integrity, awareness, and consciousness have replaced money as what is most valued.*

- *Business openly recognizes the assumption that we are all one, are interconnected, and affect each other.*

- *Business actively includes the whole person.*

- *Businesses and individuals no longer use litigation so freely. Conflicts are resolved face to face. We finally eliminate the old "legal system" and establish a system based on fairness, equality, and justice.*

- *People take off work when they want to—no one is being abused, so no one will abuse. Most people work two to three days per week, so the need to take days off is practically eliminated.*

- *There is dignity and opportunity for all—the "American dream" finally becomes a reality.*

- *Everyone has the basics—food, shelter, health care, dignity, self-respect, and the opportunity for growth.*

- *Each individual's internal growth is recognized as his or her primary purpose.*

- *The prizes in this world aren't cars, cash, trips—they are personal growth, learned lessons, awareness, consciousness, experiences, and understanding.*

- *Profits are a less dominating force in business.*

- *Money is only one means of exchange. Bartering and trading are two examples of alternative ways of conducting transactions.*

- *There are no victims. Each person, business, and community is 100 percent responsible for itself.*

- *The higher good has priority, and out of that we all prosper. Transportation companies create electric cars, and new high-tech tools for organic farming are created by companies that make chemicals. A company is willing to go out of business if it has outgrown its usefulness.*

- *Each community governs itself, and business plays an active and leading role in that process.*

- *Everyone is entitled to the same amount of time off, what we call "vacation" today—at least one month per year. Some people may choose to "work" during these periods anyway.*

- *It is recognized by all that each individual does everything for his or her own experience. This includes coming to work.*

- *It would never occur to a business to defile or deceive any person or the environment.*

- *All businesses, people, and communities are connected— part of a "global community." We can finally begin to truly act globally.*

Farfetched? In 1952, on the island of Koshima, scientists studying a species of Japanese monkey, *Macaca fusteuta*, introduced raw sweet potatoes into their diet. The sweet potatoes were dropped into the sand, and, while the monkeys liked the potatoes, they disliked the sand and dirt. An eighteen-month-old female, Imo, discovered that she could wash the potatoes in a nearby stream. She taught her mother and her playmates to do the same thing, and they, in turn, taught their mothers. Between 1952 and 1958, *all* the *young* monkeys learned to wash their dirty sweet potatoes. The adults who imitated their children learned to wash their potatoes. The rest of the older monkeys endured the dirt on their potatoes.

Then, in the autumn of 1958, one more monkey learned the task (the exact number is uncertain), and a phenomenon occurred—by that evening, *almost every monkey was washing his or her sweet potatoes.* Then an even more amazing thing happened. Colonies of monkeys on other islands that had never before seen anyone washing sweet potatoes began washing theirs. And so the "Hundredth Monkey" phenomenon was born.

The Hundredth Monkey theory, then, says that when a certain number or percentage of people achieve an awareness, that awareness spreads from mind to mind without teaching or direct contact between individuals.

The challenge is to believe in something not clearly attainable, yet obviously better. In 1971, my personal challenge was to believe that I could walk again—to have 100 percent intention and commitment to walking again, without a clear idea as to how that could happen. Though I had many setbacks, my intention remained steadfast.

Our collective challenge, I believe, is to create a world that many might call Utopia—a nice but impossible dream.

I believe we can and do create our own reality. If you could create yours, what would it be?

A Personal Exercise

What follows is an individual experience. I recommend that you read the entire process before beginning. Allow about fifteen minutes to complete it.

In a quiet environment and sitting in a comfortable position, take several deep breaths. With each inhalation, breathe in your hopes and desires. With each exhalation, release any limitations getting in the way of your expanding beyond what you already know.

Next, pull into clear focus your personal vision—how you see yourself, your life, and the world in which you live. With each breath, release the parts of your vision and the feelings that you would eliminate from your "utopia." Then, begin to replace these with thoughts and feelings that you want to experience.

Hold your personal vision as long as is comfortable. Feel it thoroughly. Do not judge. Replace your daily fears, heartbreaks, and hopelessness with these expanding thoughts and feelings.

If you care to, write down your personal vision and add to it whenever you desire. What follows is a list of questions to stimulate your thinking:

1. *Do I pay attention to my own personal growth first?*

2. *Do I resent how I spend any of my time?*

3. *To what extent am I motivated by money? What am I willing to do, or not do, because of money?*

4. *How much time do I spend alone? When I am alone, what do I do? Do I nurture and replenish myself? Do I feel lonely?*

5. *How often is my mind truly quiet?*

6. *Is my personal best enough? For everyone I associate with? For myself?*

7. *Must I be the best, at the top, number one?*

8. *Do I put my job before my family or myself?*

9. *How do I feel when I see a homeless or hungry person?*

10. *Do I consume more than I need?*

11. *Do I have less than I want?*

12. *Do I deserve the best? Can I have everything I want? What about* every *human being—can they?*

13. *Is there enough for all of us?*

Part Four

Openness, Intuition, and the Process of Change

Creativity at Work
Cheryl Harrison

Intuition in the Midst of Change:
A Key to Success in Business
Mitani D'Antien

New Listening: Key to Organizational Transformation
Barbara Fittipaldi

Seven Keys to Conscious Leadership
Sabina Spencer

The authors in this part focus on the inner processes that they have found to be of value as they have worked with change in their personal lives, their businesses, and society—on the inner work of creating openness in work relationships, where intuition can flourish and positive change can be supported.

To be open to the changing circumstances and needs of your business is a major challenge. Cheryl Harrison shares a personal example of how she followed her heart through unknown territory in developing her design business. Working in a creative field requires flexibility and openness with and between employees. She shares the steps used in developing the collaborative spirit that has contributed to her firm's success.

Intuition used to be considered a "code word" that many people used as a sort of litmus test to gauge someone's interest in spiritual development, especially in a business setting. If the other person didn't flinch at the term, it might be safe to proceed to explore other dimensions of thought. Intuition is more openly discussed these days, which makes it important to understand its meaning and application in business situations. Mitani D'Antien gives us practical examples of the use of intuition in the workplace along with exercises she teaches in her executive leadership development classes. In times of change, it's important to be able to rely on our inner knowing—our intuition—when making decisions.

Genuine listening is another important tool, and Barbara Fittipaldi helps us understand the various levels of listening, the importance of "hearing" another person, and the dangers of "automatic listening." She says that when we are so caught up in what we already know that we are unable to listen to new ideas, we limit available possibilities. "We don't have to wonder about or inquire into what is possible," she tells us; "we've got our answers, never noticing that it is what we already know that is suffocating us."

As the other authors call for new ways of nurturing the human spirit, Sabina Spencer focuses on conscious leadership, reminding us that insecurity in business and society is leading people to an "inner search." Conscious leadership, she says, "is based on the assumption that if anyone loses, no one really wins, because there is no 'us and them' anymore."

Cheryl Harrison is the founder, president, and creative director of Harrison Design Group. She has fourteen years of professional design experience in marketing, advertising, packaging, and print and graphic communications.

Harrison won San Francisco's 1985 Woman Entrepreneur of the Year Award and has been highly recognized for her professional contributions to the San Francisco Chamber of Commerce, the Business Arts Council, and the Printing Industries of Northern California. After receiving her bachelor of science degree in environmental design from the University of California at Davis, she worked in Scandinavia to develop, design, and market products for the U.S. market. Under her leadership, Harrison Design Group continues to receive national and international awards of design excellence.

Harrison Design Group's corporate clients range from Levi Strauss & Company, Pacific Telesis, and Wells Fargo Bank to Williams-Sonoma, Bank of America, and AT&T. Harrison is a frequent guest speaker at business and design seminars.

12

Creativity at Work

Cheryl Harrison

I went to work as an art director for an advertising agency right out of school. Six months later, the person I had replaced decided to rejoin the agency, and I was let go. The next day, I started my own graphics firm. That was in 1980. The business grew slowly, but steadily. In 1985, I was chosen San Francisco's Woman Entrepreneur of the Year by the Chamber of Commerce. By 1988, as president and creative director of Harrison Design Group, I was at the top of a traditional pyramid structure that had evolved as the business grew to fourteen people. And I was miserable.

******

I had a couple of senior management people under me, then all the designers, below them the production staff, and then the administrative staff. But all roads led to me. And before long, I found that I was getting pretty frenetic. The structure didn't give me any time to work out important design decisions with my designers. It didn't allow me time to think or just to put things on the back burner. Rather than being proactive, I was reacting to problems. I had to react to things rather than thinking ahead and steering them in the right direction.

More and more, with this kind of organizational structure, I found communication breaking down. Clearly, participation in the creative process was stifled from the bottom up. The administrative staff couldn't possibly be creative in their jobs, because they didn't understand the context. They were isolated. Even the best designers were isolated, because they didn't understand the business side. They didn't necessarily have a hands-on feeling—if they went over budget or spent too many hours on a project, they had no idea what that really meant, what the consequences were. Some of the smallest decisions were ultimately left up to me.

I didn't have the solution, but I knew that things weren't working the way I wanted them to. Finally, I asked myself, Where is all this going? And my conclusion was that the business was only going to get bigger, only going to get more frenetic, and I just wasn't going to be able to handle it. It certainly wasn't going to be fun anymore. It was already pretty stressful. The creative product was suffering. We weren't rising to new levels. Clients started calling and saying, "Cheryl, we like working with you, but we haven't seen you in a long time. Where are you?" That was a signal for change.

******

I had no clue what the solution was. For the moment, I just stopped. I went to different consultants—even a financial consultant who had worked with a number of other design firms. I thought he might be able to suggest a different way to structure my business or something. I took the few available courses I could find. I talked with everybody I could. None said, "Cheryl, this is the answer."

I finally decided that the best way to regroup was to do it more or less from ground zero. So as people decided to leave the firm, I simply didn't hire replacements. Toward the end of this attrition process, I let one person go.

******

Shelli was very much a part of that major change effort, that transition period. She came in for a first interview at the office and said, "I realize that you have posted a position for an administrative employee with senior level experience, and I'm pretty much just out of school, but I'm still interested in the job." And I said, "I really need someone with a lot more experience. Because of what we need to do here and where we need to go, I'm not going to be able to do it alone. I'm going to do it with one other person who must have years of experience." She came back the next day for a second interview, and at the end of the interview, she said, "I really think you should give me a chance." That threw me completely. But I thought to myself, anyone who's this determined... So I said, "Why don't we try something for about two weeks, because I have someone going on vacation. You could fill in there."

She learned so fast and picked up things so beautifully that within days she was contributing to the office and coming up with new solutions. She just moved right ahead. She asked really good questions. She was very thoughtful, but she challenged the status quo. And she became one of the most fully dimensional employees that I've ever had. She understood the administrative functions. She saw their relationship to the business. She took that to the next step and said, "I'm enjoying working on the computer. Could I use it to do some design work?" She started learning the creative side. Then she asked if she could go on some printers' press checks. She learned all about printing from outside reps who serviced our account. She asked if she could take some evening classes. She embraced the computer, the technology, and encouraged me to buy more programs for the Mac. Sure, she came up against problems, but she found solutions. They didn't faze her. She didn't let herself get upset about them.

After about a year, there was a period when Shelli and I were the only people left, when we ran the entire office. What was fascinating was that the work load remained almost the same. And it occurred to me, "How did we go from fourteen people down to two people, and we're still handling so much business?"

Yes, we were more selective about the business we took on. We were careful about how we organized that business, how we organized our time. But the most shocking part of it all was how efficient just the two of us were.

By the middle of 1992—with Shelli as a prototype employee—we were handling almost the same volume of business with just *five* on staff as we had been with *fourteen* employees in 1988.

******

In retrospect, I believe that the traditional pyramid organizational structure (see below) has failed us by pigeonholing responsibilities and capabilities and pinpointing exactly what someone's tasks should be during the day. This structured road map inevitably gets you demerits for not doing your job. And it's counterproductive to the creative process.

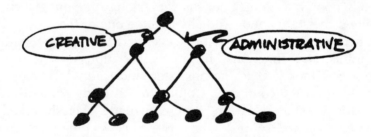

Figure 1: Pyramid Structure

There was also a perplexing notion about information—somehow, I was the only one who had it, at the top. So I decided to build a centralized administrative system in which everyone would have access to all critical information, and everyone would contribute to the administration through whatever they were working on. From the process of conceptual design to project implementation, each designer in our group is now involved in the whole comprehensive notion of a project, not just an isolated element of it. The skills required to work in this way are different, but I feel that the results are far more successful.

In the past, one designer would take almost full responsibility for a particular client and a particular project, and my job was to keep each designer focused in the right direction. But now I feel that we all are taking responsibility for the joys and the disappointments, the good and the bad, the success or failure of each project. We all really feel that.

Today, I allow people to take on a lot more responsibility. Access to information and direct participation are the key—through the use of the computer, certainly, but also involving everyone much earlier on in the process. We work very collaboratively in the office to prepare for a client presentation so that everyone really knows what's going on. If the baton needs to be passed or the pendulum needs to swing—this person is now going to take a little more responsibility on this project and a little less responsibility over here—everybody's very comfortable doing that. And if someone's on vacation, no problem. We can handle it.

How did we get to this point? Let me reminisce.

******

The first computer in the office—an IBM clone—was like this black cloud, initially. It was *not* positively received in our creative environment.

What happened with that first computer experience—something that I realized years later—was that we became very detail oriented and very administratively oriented because we had a new tool available to track all these "business" things. But it started to detract from what we were in the business of doing, which was the creative product. The computer soon became all-consuming in its ability to take over administrative functions. It was such a challenge just to figure out how it was going to meet our wishes that we spent a lot of energy in that area—too much energy.

201

We broke this stranglehold with the introduction of the Macintosh as our right-hand creative tool, available to everyone. Fortunately, this time, it became a creative tool *first*, and *then* an administrative tool.

The designers can now relate to the complete creative, production, and implementation process by the unique nature of the Macintosh. Very early in the creative process, we put our design projects up on the computer. What followed was a fluid evolution of that design or that concept through to completion. Formerly, three or four different people worked to accomplish this same task. Now one person can carry a project through to completion. It's a very different type of person—one who has strong conceptual skills but also has implementation and management skills—who can envision how something would *really* be produced and how that design would successfully work once it was printed and implemented.

******

I think that the new organizational structure that is evolving—I see it as a flat circle—has a lot to do with one-on-one communications and access to information: information to determine what's important and what's not, what's possible and what's not, what the priorities, and project objectives are. It's core information—so that people can keep their own work, their own passion in the proper context.

I'm discovering that the best communication between people working in a collaborative environment is communication that's not really planned, when there's an informality in how people interact. To have people actually schedule meetings at various points in time is okay. But what seems to work best is when someone has an idea and I can just pop right over and we can look at it together—right then.

I try to create an atmosphere in which I make myself available to people as they need me. In a creative endeavor, it's hard to know when you're going to get to that critical point—at 1:00 P.M. or 3:15 P.M. or whenever. The way I'm trying to work is to say, "I'm going to be here from 1:00 to 5:00 this afternoon, so if you reach a point where we need to get together, anytime during that window is fine."

My approach is also to say, "Check in with me when you're at a point of needing to get away from an idea." It may not be complete, and it's fine if it's not yet perfect. In fact, I don't need to see the project when it's perfect. If it's perfect, then don't show it to me at all. When you need air space, when you've been so close to this thing that you just need to get some time away, do it. When you're thinking, "I need a new opinion, I need to bring this to another level, I need to figure out a way to look at this differently to see whether I like it or don't like it, to see whether it's working," then I want people to come to me. But I come to them for the same reason. I need *them* sometimes more than they need me.

One thing I've learned during this transitional process is that the collaborative spirit of working out a problem together is heightened when nobody has to report to anyone. People are responsible for themselves. They have information, so they can find out what's going on. They don't have to waste time on typical office protocol. I don't have to scold anyone for being over budget or late for work. Everybody knows where things stand.

Within the structure of the office, I have been amazed to find out that people who thought that they were production-oriented ended up being great designers. People who came in with strong administrative skills ended up being some of the best conceptual thinkers. Suddenly, I found that when people who thought that they had very defined skills were given the opportunity to cross all parts of the process, they rose to the occasion and came up with ideas that offered a totally new, fresh perspective that contributed greatly to the end result. I call this structure the kinetic circle (see diagram next page).

Today, no one person's idea is any better than any other's. This is a big item. In the former structure, I had the final say. People would wait to meet with me, and then what I said would go. It would frustrate the living daylights out of me. I'd say,

"Why do you guys think that just because I said this or that, it's the way you necessarily have to go? It is not the case. Your idea is as good as mine." They wouldn't believe me.

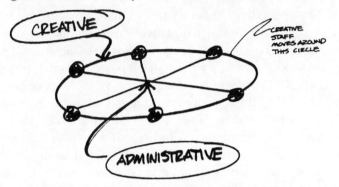

Figure 2: Diagram of the Kinetic Circle

******

However, in the kinetic-circle concept, people evolve their own ideas, bouncing them off me or, if I'm not there, if I'm out of town, doing it together, among themselves. There is no judgment of whether it's good, bad, or indifferent. Everybody knows that they can run something by a few other people in the office and then come to an even a better decision.

Whether or not I agree with it in the end, I know that people thought it through to the best of their ability, that they used one another as a resource to get to the best point, and so I will always support them in their decision—unquestionably. And they know that. That's a very important notion. It's one of the biggest realizations that I've had—that I can trust people who work with me to come up with solutions equal to my own. It is a trust that is now very deep. It's a trust whereby I can walk away from something that I might have a lot of anxiety about and know that it's going to be taken care of. And that's an incredible feeling. It's an even more incredible feeling to come back and see how well something was solved—often much better than I could have done myself. It's an implicit trust—that I don't even need to question people's capability.

A lot of this is about freeing me up but also, in the process, freeing everyone up.

******

Now, when I hire someone new into the office, I like to give them a very big, multidimensional project. Typically, it involves design, a conceptual visual component, and client communication. It has management, production, and follow-through, requiring a whole spectrum of talents, tasks, and demands. It's a small enough project that, if some part doesn't go quite right, the patching up of some minor stumbling block is not going to be a problem. But what that project will tell me, and what it shows to the rest of the office, is how this person thinks—where they can run with something and where they hesitate, where they feel confident and where they flounder, where they're efficient and where they waste time. And I think that it's also a feedback mechanism for the new employee as well—sometimes very painful, because they're given so much responsibility so early.

I've met so many people who have said, "Cheryl, you're so lucky to be a creative person," and then in the same breath, they'll say, "I wish I were more creative." And I just feel like saying, "But you are!" I believe that every one of us has a huge creative potential. It's just that something happened when we were growing up, someone told us, "You don't know how to draw," or "You don't know how to write," or "You don't know how to play piano." And all of a sudden, we shut off that creative part of ourselves.

Our lives could be so much richer and so much more interesting if we just realized that we do have the capability to think differently—maybe to change the way we've done something, or to be a little bit more resourceful, or to find a different way of doing something. In our day-to-day lives, there are different options that may have even greater value that we're overlooking because we're used to doing it the same way. The greatest inventions and innovations often come from taking something that has existed in one area forever and putting it somewhere else. People say, "Isn't that just brilliant!" It's not

205

necessarily that it was so brilliant or so unique. It was just that someone thought to look at it upside down and put it in a different context.

People have capabilities far beyond what they think they have. They are hired for a particular job but, given the opportunity, they end up being capable of so much more. They can contribute to the end result in areas no one, including themselves, ever believed they could.

******

Recently, I was thinking about the times when we've been in a crunch to design something, to create something from scratch, and we've had no boundaries. Actually, it's more difficult to create something when there are no walls, no boundaries whatsoever. Part of creative thinking is learning how to use the walls to guide you to a solution. People immediately look at the walls and don't look at the path created between the walls. Or they don't realize that they can reorient the walls. It has to do with observation of one's own thinking. In fact, walls and problems, issues and dilemmas, differing opinions, budget constraints, and other things that seem to get in the way can end up helping us to create the ideal solution.

It saddens me to think that many people in the workplace today really don't realize that they can move those walls. They do not believe that they can work with the people who are sitting right next to them, right across the desk from them, in the next office, or down the hall—or someone they meet in the elevator—that they can work with that person in some way just to run an idea by them, to get to the next level. Rather, people worry about what some other person will think.

Communication with co-workers can help all of us elevate a project to a new dimension. It doesn't matter what the person says. What matters is that they have a comment and they have an opinion. That opinion or observation, perfect or not, usually allows us to leverage yet another opinion on top of another. We would then, almost through a creative dialogue, evolve to a new, fresh approach. Whether or not we would evolve it into something that would ultimately work, who really cares at that point? In this dialogue, a solution evolves faster than if I just sat there alone and tried to stew in my own ideas.

******

As there are budget cuts across the board, as the economy sputters, as competition increases and the pace of change becomes exponential, we need to become more efficient in the workplace. We need to think more clearly. We can't be as wasteful. There's a sense of responsibility today. It's almost like caring for the ecology of the workplace, the balance of positive and negative. And I think that we have to be significantly more efficient with our own resources—ourselves, the people we work with, the things we work with—and more conscious of the waste that we might create in time and materials.

If we can find ways to inspire our human capabilities in the workplace, I think we might supersede what we ever thought we could do in many other aspects of our lives. And one way we might do this is by understanding how we think, how we create, how we problem solve, and how we can also work together with others.

The workplace has so much to offer, now more than ever before, because people are working together toward furthering common goals. Look at how much time we spend in the workplace today. With that dedication, there's an opportunity. With our enhanced relationships with co-workers, and better understanding of ourselves, we're all working to make a contribution to that entity, that company, that thing. And that entity, that thing, has a valued relationship to a greater world as well.

******

I don't yet know how to grow a business ten times our size, based on the kinetic-circle concept, other than to think about a model that might have many satellites; a model with a lot of small groups making up the whole.

That will be the subject of my next essay.

207

Mitani D'Antien, Ph.D., has more than two decades of experience as an educator, consultant, and healer in the San Francisco Bay Area. Her Intuition Development for Professionals intensive training programs teach participants to strengthen their intuition and to increase results-oriented applications for the workplace. She is committed to a view of the future in which intuition is the bridge to excellent management and corporate renewal.

D'Antien works with CEOs, senior executives, and other professionals from such companies as Ford, McKesson, Wells Fargo Bank, Bank of America, Citibank, Alcoa, and PG&E to access their inner strengths and consolidate their success with personal ethics and a powerful healing impact. In addition to consultation services, lectures, and corporate training, she has produced workbooks and audiotape packages dealing with aspects of leading a successful life consonant with full potential. She also appears frequently on national radio and television.

13

Intuition in the Midst of Change: A Key to Success in Business

Mitani D'Antien

No one would dispute that we have entered a decade of sweeping changes. Poised on the edge of the greatest potential for renewed growth and expansive success, we are faced with an equal possibility of stagnation. Some are drawn by the pull to forge new pathways, making quantum leaps through inspired leadership, exceptional management skills, and well-defined strategic plans. From a solid core of discernment and clarity, these new leaders combine hard data with intuitive hunches to carve out better lives for themselves and those they work with.

As the bureaucratic structures and old ways of doing business begin to crumble, some feel frightened and succumb to feeling hopeless and overwhelmed. The news and economic indicators seem to reinforce their worst fears. Sometimes the very gravity of the problems masks the great potential for something new to arise.

Whether we are frightened by the crumbling of the old or inspired by the promise of the future, these times call for sweeping changes, and change we must.

Nature gives us a reassuring way to look at change. Every winter in Maine, where I grew up, layer after layer of crusty ice builds up on the ponds. The fish and frogs burrow into the mud at the bottom, as life in the pond becomes dormant.

Maine winters can seem to be endless, and we can lose faith that spring will ever come. Yet each year, spring returns, and the warming rays of the sun melt the ice. Finally, just a thin crust of ice floats in the center of the pond. One day, without warning, the ice drops as the water at the bottom rushes to the top. The whole pond is reoxygenated. The frogs and fish come to life and swim again. Life is renewed in the pond.

Something else happens, though. The silt from the bottom disperses throughout the water. The bottom is not visible. The pond looks muddy and murky, as if nothing could ever live or grow there. But with time, the silt settles, revealing tadpoles and tiny fish.

Just as the greatest potential for new life in the pond is disguised by the murkiness, so it is with change in our local, corporate, and global ponds when life begins to stagnate and we have frozen into old patterns. Eventually, we are called upon to do something new. Yet change brings a period of chaos. Frightened, some submit to the chaos, allowing external factors to control their reactions. The economy, the CEO, and the manager are seen as controllers of fate. Those who lose perspective, succumbing to the angst associated with change, can endanger their jobs if their performance level drops.

What about the person who is able to hold a positive vision of the future in the midst of the murkiness of the chaos? That person is self-reliant, able to think on his or her feet, creative and decisive. Acting from a reliable core of discernment and clarity, that person exudes confidence and inspires others to excel. Living their values and principles, vision holders operate from a base of analysis combined with intuition.

Intuition is an inner resource, "a power," according to Webster, "to know without recourse to reasoning." In uncertain times, when old systems are breaking down, intuition becomes an invaluable key to unlocking future successes. As the noted futurist Willis Harman (1991) posits in the first chapter of *New Traditions in Business*, "Developing intuitive leadership in the future will not be a luxury or a passing fad; it will be the heart of business. The challenges will be great.... Intuition is a code word for a necessary transformation of business—indeed, of global society."

Is intuition a special gift endowed only on a privileged few? As little as five years ago, corporate executives insisted upon decision-making practices based on facts, figures, and hard data. According to the director of organization development of a Fortune 100 company, the prevailing attitude now is that intuition gives the "big picture." Many CEOs are finding that for some decisions, they can never gather enough hard data and are relying on their intuition, usually called their "gut instinct," to make decisions. Although some people feel that they have always been intuitive, intuition is actually a skill that can be developed and fostered.

Intuition can enhance decision making and managerial strategy. In a paper prepared for the International Management Development International (IMDI) Roundtable in Lusanne, Switzerland, Karen Wilhelm-Buckley (1988) suggests that intuitive leaders use intuition as an early warning system, to foresee the best timing for impending changes, to sense leverage points in systems as they come into focus, and to anticipate opportunities before they become public.

The following stories illustrate what intuition has accomplished.

- *A mid-level manager in a corporate planning function initially had little influence on the strategic direction chosen by upper-level management. However, he accessed intuitive information: what was important for the company to anticipate, when to bring information out, and whom to approach first. Consequently, within a year, he was invited to participate in executive group strategy planning retreats.*

- *An executive with a Fortune 500 company recognized that to advance her career, she needed to move on. Using her intuition, she prepared her list of criteria for the new job, deciding that she wanted the new job to find her rather than going out looking for it. Within one month, she received five leads, one of which matched her criteria perfectly. Within six months on the new job, she was promoted to senior vice-president.*

- *A vice-president, newly hired to turn around sales and service results, used her intuition to engage the partnership in building an innovative package of programs and processes and to discover the best way to gain senior management approval. Within one year, the company became known for legendary service: a 20 percent improvement in customer satisfaction with a corresponding 22 percent increase in sales.*

There are two important cornerstones for developing a firm, reliable foundation for the safe, responsible use of intuition: *grounding* and a code of ethics. Let's start with grounding.

Grounding is the ability to be fully present and responsive to people and events while using intuition. The grounded person is innovative, trustworthy, responsible, and reliable. The grounded person makes accurate assessments, is productive, follows through with persistence, and meets deadlines.

Personal and organizational disaster can result when we are not grounded in using intuition or solid in our code of ethics. Once an entrepreneur came to me for help after she had taken a form of intuition training in which she had not been taught to use intuition appropriately. She wrongfully used personal information that she had intuited about friends and clients and proceeded to enlighten each of them with her insights. Trespassing others' right to privacy, this entrepreneur lost her business and had to spend years rebuilding. Some customers and friends were lost forever. She had not built in the internal controls that are necessary for accuracy and discernment. She learned the hard way what can happen when you are not grounded and following a code of ethics.

We have all worked with ungrounded people occasionally. They are easy to spot as they go around in circles, looking overwhelmed and dropping pieces of paper. Ungrounded people are clumsy, have little accidents, and are forgetful. Over the phone, their voices sound tired, high-pitched, impatient, and demanding. They misinterpret information and create extra work for themselves and others.

Being ungrounded is like standing with your feet tightly together and your knees locked. If someone hit you on the shoulder while you are standing this way, you would most likely lose your balance and stumble. Being grounded is like standing with your feet about a foot apart and your knees slightly bent. If the same push came along, you could move out of the way and allow it to move past you, or you could use the force to your advantage and send it back. Being grounded, you automatically have options. You maintain your balance when grounded, no matter what comes your way. Grounding becomes your foundation for further growth and excellence.

Being grounded and centered is essential for developing intuition that you can rely on and feel comfortable and safe using. Years ago, Benjamin Franklin developed lightning rods. These rods are placed around a house and set firmly in the ground, protruding up above the roof of the house. When a bolt of lightning is directed toward the house, the lightning rods pick up the electrical energy and grounds it into the earth, saving the house from the full impact of the powerful bolt. This grounding allows houses to safely weather otherwise dangerous lightning storms. People can use a similar type of grounding technique to enable themselves to function more effectively when using intuition in the workplace or in their everyday lives.

A group of senior executives from a Fortune 100 company cited this grounding technique as the single most important skill that they learned in the training I offer, Intuition Development for Professionals. They felt that grounding was absolutely essential for the responsible use of intuition. The following technique, which can be used in the privacy of your home or office, provides a way to obtain and maintain a solid, grounded foundation for intuition.

1. Find a comfortable location. When you begin, find a comfortable sitting position, loosening your belt if you need to. Place your feet firmly on the floor about a foot apart with your knees resting comfortably above your feet. Place your hands palms down on your thighs and gently close your eyes.

2. Allow yourself to relax. Raise your shoulders as high as you can, tense them for thirty seconds, and then drop them. Take a deep breath and raise your shoulders again. Hold your breath and tense the shoulders even tighter this time. Then exhale and let your shoulders drop. Move your shoulders around in a circle, back and forth.

   Allow your breath to return to normal and notice how your shoulders feel now. As you take the next deep breath, tense each part of your body, from the feet to the calves and all the way up through the hands, torso, shoulders, neck, and head. As you exhale, imagine your breath traveling from your head down to your feet. Repeat, and this time roll the tension all the way up and even tighten your face. Exhale and release all the tension from your body; let it drain into the earth. Return your breathing to normal and get a sense of the way your body feels now. Notice any spots that may still be holding tension, and breathe into them.

3. Visualize a grounding cord attached to the base of your spine. Now shift your awareness to this cord. Inhale deeply. Then exhale fully into this grounding cord, like the lightning rod, extending to the center of the earth. Once again, inhale deeply and

214

exhale, making your grounding cord denser and stronger. With your breath, send two similar cords from the base of your spine through your legs and feet into the earth. Return your breath to normal, and visualize the strengthening earth energy flowing through your grounding cords. Allow the earth energy to fill each cell of your body. Take a moment to compare the way you feel now to the way you felt when you began this exercise. Open your eyes gently, feeling refreshed and recharged.

When you are first learning the grounding exercise, it is a good idea to practice the technique slowly on a daily basis. As the procedure becomes more familiar, you will be able to re-establish your grounding in stressful situations just by taking a silent deep breath.

Once your grounding is firmly in place, it is time to lay down the other cornerstone of your foundation for the safe use of intuition: your code of ethics. A group of top level managers in another course, Advanced Intuition Training for Professionals, outlined the following ten guidelines that can help you assess your principles as you structure your personal code of ethics:

1. Check personal grounding constantly to ensure the integrity of intuition.

2. Be sensitive to individual and organizational needs and have a sense of timeliness.

3. Choose appropriate times and places for practicing and building intuitive skills.

4. Curb impulses to manipulate for personal gain at the expense of others.

5. Assess the impact of intuitive insights on yourself and others.

6. Avoid forcing or exploiting situations or other people.

7. Verify intuitive insights when possible and check them *against common sense.*

8. Establish procedures for reviewing intuitive work with others to assess whether it is on or off the track.

9. Respect and embrace the diversity of co-workers and the organization.

10. Follow conscious and explicit ethical standards.

At a conference exploring intuition in the workplace, one participant asked, "When I am using my intuition, how do I know I am right?" This is an important question indeed. Intuition used correctly is both accurate and reliable, but we must be able to recognize the cues that let us know we are on the right track. Just as a salesperson must have a successful track record, our intuition must be based on a track record of reliability.

The surest way to develop intuition is to go more slowly rather than faster. Fear inhibits intuition. So does pressure to perform. Studies of runners show definitive results. Running or jogging for pleasure produces a rush of endorphins, a pleasurable relaxation response. As soon as the runner begins training for competition, however, the flow of endorphins is often blocked.

I have found the following step-by-step method to be beneficial in building a reliability track record. This method establishes an internal monitoring system of discernment by developing a relationship with the subconscious. Both those who are just starting out and those who are now teaching others to use their intuition, have found this technique valuable.

1. *Allow yourself to enter a grounded, relaxed state.* Use the grounding technique above. Whenever we enter a relaxed state, we are in touch with our subconscious.

2. *Hold a conversation with your subconscious.* Let your subconscious know that you want to work with it to develop reliable intuition skills and describe the steps that follow. Reassure your subconscious that you will work at its pace, since it knows the correct pace for your develop-

216

ment. Allowing the subconscious to set the pace of your training and conversing with gentleness lead to outcomes that are fulfilling.

3. *Choose a symbol to represent "yes."* Your symbol should be one that you feel comfortable with and that is easily recognizable. A symbol can be visual, auditory, or kinesthetic; for instance, the proverbial "light bulb" representing a brilliant idea, the "ting" sound emitted when a crystal glass is tapped, or shivers up the spine.

4. *Train your symbol to arise accurately.* Make a list of ten true statements; for instance, "My name is ___." Tell your symbol that it represents the answer "yes" and instruct it to appear after each true statement. Let your symbol know that it has performed accurately.

   Then make a list of ten false statements, again keeping them simple and direct. As you read each false statement, notice that your "yes" symbol does not arise.

   At this stage of the process, you are reassuring your subconscious by posing question statements to which you already know the answers. This provides the foundation for the next step.

5. *Make the transition to greater risk.* During this phase, spend a few minutes each morning making simple statements about the way your day will go. When you first begin this phase, it is important to make statements about events that you know will occur. As your accuracy rate rises, you can increase the level of difficulty by making statements that include your best hunches. Write down your results. At the end of the day, review your list to check for accuracy and acknowledge your success.

   As you access your answers, note any feelings of tightness in your body. You may have stopped breathing, tightened your pelvis, or squinted your eyes. These are signals that you are trying to control the answers to your questions. Controlled answers do not come from a place of clarity within yourself. Intuition occurs when we are

217

relaxed and breathing freely. Soon you will learn to recognize the neutral state of being in which intuition thrives.

6. *Determine the length of the process.* One way to determine the length of the preceding phases is to use your "yes" symbol technique. This is a way for your subconscious to reveal to you the pace that is most conducive to your growth.

Another way to track your progress is a linear approach of scoring your results. If you pose ten questions per day, with each accurate answer earning ten points, you can derive a percentage of accuracy, which I call your Reliability Quotient. Once you have maintained 90 percent or better for several days, you can move to the next level of difficulty with confidence. If your accuracy rate drops at the next level, take the time to go back and lay a more firm foundation.

7. *Trust your intuition in the moment.* In this phase, you are beginning to live your intuitive faculties rather than consciously practicing the steps. However, if you are in doubt about an intuitive hunch, you can ask your subconscious to work with you to access accurate information with the help of your "yes" symbol.

During the step-by-step training program, you build a stable foundation of confidence in your intuitive abilities. You learn to recognize the visual, auditory, or kinesthetic cues that let you know you are on the right track. Developing the ability to recognize cues creates a strong internal center. Your intuition thrives because you provided an environment of appreciation.

One of the ways that we can foster continued growth is to modify step 5. With this technique, rather than intuiting how your day will go, you decide what you *want* to have happen, and acknowledge yourself when it has occurred. I call this the Good Stories technique. It is important to start with small outcomes. Here are some examples of good stories from the beginning phase: the friend you wanted to hear from calls; the small piece of chocolate that you wanted arrives with the lunch check. Again, over time, you build a track record of small successes, eventually shifting to greater wins. Day by day, your world becomes a reflection of your internal confidence in your intuition.

The vice-president of sales and service with one of the largest banks in the world noted the positive effect of relating her good stories to others during the Intuition Development for Professionals training and brought the technique to her very conservative company. At the close of her weekly staff meetings, each person told a small corporate "win" that they had had during the week. By sharing their wins, her team built a context of success. Because their wins were acknowledged and appreciated, each staff member took greater responsibility for performing his or her tasks with excellence. Eventually, when her company began downsizing, eliminating whole departments, her team continued to be recognized for producing stellar successes.

Another story illustrates that you get more of what you pay attention to. When the economy began to decline, two external organizational development consultants feared that their contracts would dry up. One focused outside of herself to obtain data to allay her fears. However, news reports and the rumor mill confirmed her worst fears about the job market and the state of the economy. Within months, her contracts had indeed dried up. The other faced her fears head on and cleared them out. Then she replicated the relaxed state that she had often obtained during her intuition training. Using the "yes" technique, she accessed information regarding the state of her business, as well as information useful to the companies with which she was consulting. Not only were her contracts extended, but the companies reaped large benefits as well.

Look at the difference between these two approaches. One woman focused outside herself and generated her reality on the basis of fear and insecurity. Because the economy was shaky, she created shakiness in her own life. The other acknowledged that there was a reality outside of herself that was shaky and that this reality made her afraid. But, by acknowledging her fear, she moved her fears aside so that she could get a clear perspective on the situation. Then she generated contracts based on the degree of her internal security. In her life and the lives of those she worked with, the "economy" improved.

As we develop intuition step by step, we begin to fuse a unique style that can be relied upon. Then we can use our intuition in a larger scope, knowing with confidence that we will be accurate and will enhance the experience of those we work with.

An internal organization development consultant I work with had developed her intuition over time and used the grounding exercises daily. She was to lead a facilitation for a group of thirty supervisors, which included a manager who had become isolated and fearful and was attacking her colleagues and staff. When my client (I will call her Susan) arrived at the seminar room, the alienated woman sat right in the front row to her right side. As the facilitation went along, the alienated manager began to attack Susan. Susan remained grounded while working to reintegrate the manager into the group. In the afternoon, the alienated manager stood up, pounded her fist, and blamed Susan for her problems. She shouted, "I'm going to take you to court for what you have done to me. I'm going to sue you," and stormed out, slamming the door behind her. Needless to say, Susan was shaken. She had just taken the brunt of the emotions that the alienated manager felt toward the whole group. What Susan really wanted to do was leave the room and recuperate from the experience, but she couldn't. Knowing that she needed to re-establish her grounding, she took a risk and asked the group, "Would you be willing to try something with me that may be very different from anything you've ever done before? I'd like to lead you on a guided meditation that may help us all to feel better."

Reluctantly the group agreed. Susan led them through the grounding process very thoroughly and slowly. Spirits lifted and courage mustered, the group began to brainstorm about how to integrate the alienated manager into the group. They adjourned the session and reconvened the next day. Even the alienated manager returned for the session. For a moment, no one spoke. Then one of the men in the group said, "I don't know what that was we did yesterday, but could we do that again, please?" The group that had formerly been reluctant now eagerly followed the grounding instructions. As soon as they finished, the group took over, using the ideas that they had brainstormed the previous day, and successfully integrated the alienated woman into the group.

The facilitator's job was very easy that day. The now integrated woman didn't sue. Her management style changed, and the management team began to cooperate in a way that they had never been able to before.

Susan took a risk that day, but she knew that she could trust her abilities. She had built a solid foundation for her intuition. When the corporate waters became muddy, she was able to perceive a way to lead the group to clarity and resolution. Through her confident leadership, the group was able to create an outcome that was far greater than their original expectations.

At this unique time in history, we each have an opportunity to choose the way we relate to the natural cycle of change. Some of us will become embroiled in the chaos, frightened and lost. Others will choose to create a solid center of discernment and clarity within. Those who develop reliable intuition skills can forge those skills into a powerful tool for creative leadership.

Barbara Fittipaldi is a partner in Landmark Consulting, an international consulting, management development, and executive education firm with offices in Somerville, New Jersey; Oakland, California; and Munich, Germany. She is also the executive director of the Center for Women, Leadership, and the Future.

Fittipaldi has been an international management consultant and program leader since 1975. In addition to consulting, she designs and leads programs and trains others to lead and consult. Her background includes degrees in chemistry, physics, and mathematics.

Mel Toomey, a partner in Landmark Consulting, and Edward M. Gurowitz, executive director of the Center for Management Design and a partner in Landmark Consulting, collaborated in writing this chapter.

14

New Listening: Key to Organizational Transformation

Barbara Fittipaldi

Bold new futures are possible for organizations and the people who work in them. Transformed organizations, or *learning organizations,* can be developed. Why, then is it so difficult to shift the current culture of an organization? What blocks innovation; what stops organizations from generating change?

There is a "superglue" that holds an organization's culture together and perpetuates "business as usual." My colleagues and I have spent the last fifteen years investigating the nature of this "superglue." There is something operating in the background of the organization that determines its fundamental culture and makes it appear nearly impossible to embrace innovation and create new futures.

Numerous reports of organizational transformation clearly demonstrate that transformation is possible. But for the most part, it is argued that this transformation is a by-product of the current circumstances rather than a result of leadership's intentions.

In their book *Breakthroughs*, Nayak and Ketteringham, studied twelve cases of organizational breakthroughs and concluded that breakthroughs or paradigm shifts cannot be planned but are a product of the circumstances. What an organization can do, they say, is stand ready for the right circumstances and then be ready to take advantage of them.

Arden Sims, CEO of Globe Metallurgical Inc., said, following that organization's eight-year transformation, "Globe found what worked—and what worked are the innovations that make today's cutting-edge companies." He later said, "The innovations were serendipitous."

There is another possibility—that what appears to be serendipity or the product of circumstances is, in fact, accessible, but only after an organization exposes a fundamental aspect of its culture that in the ordinary course of events remains unexamined.

To bring about an organizational transformation, one must first identify and get underneath the current culture and, more importantly, uncover the "superglue" that holds the current culture in place. Operating within this existing, unexamined culture at best results in improvement that is a continuation of the past. While improvement is worthwhile, even continuous improvement is not enough to meet the challenges that many organizations face in today's business climate.

How does an organization continue with what is working, see clearly what is not working, and break out of its unexamined culture or paradigm of operation to take new ground and reach new heights of success?

I suggest that we start by looking at where an organization is "located." By this, I do not mean that we look at the location of its offices, plants, or warehouses, its papers of incorporation or the minutes of its meetings, or, for that matter, its products or services. These are only artifacts that represent and symbolize the organization. I suggest that an organization is "located" in its culture and that this culture lives in conversation and, more specifically, in an aspect of conversation called "listening." It is this "listening" that forms the "superglue" of the culture, and it is already present before anyone in the organization speaks.

Automatic Listening

Let me give you an example of what I mean by the term *listening*.

Two competitive U.S. corporations were working on a joint project. The first step was to build a team composed of engineers from both companies. They were all very committed. The project was going to be profitable for both companies ($650 million over two years), and yet nothing was moving forward. It seemed that nothing could get done, and there was always a point of disagreement or argument.

When both teams were asked to think about the assumptions that they brought to their new working partnership, they started to discover some fundamental and underlying judgments, evaluations, and assessments that they had about one another, such as:

- *They are our competitors—we can't trust them.*

- *Our engineers are better than their engineers.*

- *We do things our way— the right way; they do things wrong.*

- *Whatever we do, they're going to steal.*

- *They're going to steal some of the contracts.*

- *We don't really want to work with them (after all, we've been in bidding wars with them on other projects).*

- *They are really the enemy.*

No amount of leadership could build teamwork on top of these unspoken assessments, on top of what they already *knew*. All of this is what they had already "listened" to in their own minds.

This is what I am referring to by the term *listening* or, more accurately, *automatic listening*. Once we've listened to something, it is too late! Realizing this can be a major breakthrough for people.

The more I work in the area of organizational transformation, creating learning organizations, the more convinced I am that what is already "heard" or known, before anyone speaks or acts—what we've already listened to—will shape and determine the future far more powerfully than any action taken.

I asked a client, a senior executive, for an example of "automatic listening" in her organization. She told me the following story:

> The first week in my new position, a senior vice-president in my organization called to welcome me to the division. She told me, "Pat, the first six months will be hell. There is a ritual hazing that they put women through here. You might just as well know it going in. It will go away after six months; after six months, it worked out for me, but you should just know it."
>
> I said to myself, Oh no, now I'm going to have an automatic listening for the ritual hazing. Then I asked a few people about it, and one of the guys told me that it's not just women, it happens to everyone who's new. Then I realized that the woman who told me about it had an automatic listening that it only happened to women.
>
> Some examples of the ritual hazing are that they will ignore you deliberately, or they'll ignore things that you say and then one of them will say it later and take credit for it. Or they'll joke about the division you worked for. From the moment she told me about ritual hazing, I watched and listened for it everywhere—my antennae were up, wondering when it would happen next.
>
> I wonder what work would have been like if she had never told me that, if I wasn't always looking and listening for that culture of ritual hazing.

Assumptions

These unexamined assumptions form the current culture that limits innovation and new possibilities and blocks the transformation of organizations. These assumptions are there when we join the organization, and over time, we become enculturated. This leaves us able to affect only change that is consistent with the culture rather than consistent with what is needed in a rapidly changing business landscape.

These unspoken and unexamined assumptions or paradigms (that we and those we work with have listened to before we start any endeavor) color and determine the future of our work far more than anything we have to say, anything we know, or anything we might do.

What is *critically* important to realize is that what we *"hear"* or listen to determines what we *say*, which in turn determines our *actions*, which in turn determine the *results* or the *future*.

At one major corporation, an organizational myth is that "they always kill the messenger." In other words, the bearer of bad news winds up in trouble. In the last fiscal year, all departments waited until the end of the year to announce that they were running a little bit over budget. This resulted in a budget crisis, since it was too late to do anything about it. People's behavior was driven by the underlying "myth" or assumption.

Have you ever noticed that when someone starts to say something, you already have an impression of what it will be? Even when you enter a conversation intending to be open and generous and neutral, within seconds you are reacting the way you ordinarily do. This is the mode of listening we call "automatic."

The automatic mode of listening has several dimensions, and until these dimensions are recognized, it will be difficult to identify and get underneath the current culture so that organizations are free to invent new futures. Until then, the current culture and paradigms will continue to determine the future of the organization.

Radar Metaphor

Think of these dimensions of automatic listening as if they were antennae tuned to listen in a particular way, like radar. Radar is an antenna that is very selective: it locates solid objects. What it doesn't pick up is wind, because radar beams don't bounce off wind. Radar picks up only what it is designed to pick up.

Like radar, automatic listening picks up only what it is designed to pick up. It acts as a filter that rejects what does not "fit" the current paradigm, or shapes the input so that it does fit, thereby masking or precluding any possibility outside the matrix that the listening provides. Thus, if we want to learn or create something new, and someone says something that doesn't fit with what we already know, it does not register on our radar.

We are left with an extension of what we already know, which in turn leads to improvement of what is already there rather than real innovation or breakthrough.

Let us examine these dimensions of automatic listening, this "superglue."

1. Assessments

For the most part, we are listening for: Do we agree or disagree? Do we like it or not? Is it right or wrong? Can we use it or not? and Does it fit with and confirm what we already know?

We have an opinion, an assessment, about everything. Someone says something and everyone who is listening "votes" instantly and automatically. We are automatically assessing ourselves and others *all the time*. This is not conscious and intentional; it happens without any work or effort on our part. "Voting" is going on continuously in the background of every conversation.

For example, a senior manager told me that he was beginning to recognize the listening, his antenna for assessments, and in those moments he was free to listen for "what is actually being said" or "what is here that I don't see?" Something very powerful is possible out of that kind of listening.

He then related the following incident:

A senior vice-president in my corporation issued a memo to senior management in which he said that the way we were succeeding in certain areas was accidental. As I read it, my immediate reaction was that it was accusative and derogatory. Then I found myself asking, What does he really mean by this?

And when I looked again, I saw that he was saying that we really didn't have a clear design for what we were doing. While for the most part what we were doing was successful, some of our success was accidental. His point was to draw our attention to what was missing in our design. And I said to myself, Very worthwhile statement, and I put the memo away.

I came in to work the next morning and you wouldn't have believed how upset everyone was. We must have lost at least a day of productivity from the senior people in the corporation because they were so upset about this memo—because they took it like an accusation that what they were doing was "accidental."

I realized that they were already listening "through" their assessment that he was out to criticize them. Therefore, they had to defend themselves and what they were doing.

I spoke to the manager who had sent out the memo who apologized for leaving people with that misunderstanding. He confirmed that he was not putting anyone down or accusing anyone.

Even though everyone knew that this person often said things that were a little awkward, they got upset anyway. My biggest frustration was that I was trying to communicate the opportunity in his statement to people who were upset and I could not get through to them.

If everyone in this case had seen that they were doing "automatic listening," they would have realized that their assessments were not necessarily the *truth* or the *facts*. This would have left them free to listen to what was missing or really being said, rather than listening to their assessments. This questioning would have led them to new power and new possibilities. Productivity would not have skidded to a halt, people would have taken action more quickly, and this would have encouraged others to act.

As important as it is to see how our own automatic listening colors how we hear and interpret what is happening, it is also important to see that other people are also listening in this mode.

What starts to become obvious is that we are not hearing each other at all. What we are listening to is what *we* are saying *about* what they have said. We even assess that we assess too much or have an opinion that we are too opinionated. Try to stop it, and it's already too late!

And right now we are looking into the phenomenon that we are "too late" for. Our standards and assessments about everything and everyone (how it "should" be) are in the background and *silent*, yet shaping what is possible and shaping our actions.

2. Personal

It is important to note that most people think that their assessments are *personal* assessments—they are making them individually, without the influence of others.

Part of our automatic listening is that we think, feel, and know that our opinions, our views, are ours personally—determined or controlled by us. If that is true, if your feelings are yours personally, you can simply stop having those feelings and have different ones. You could feel good all the time, for instance, if they are personal and determined by you.

Do you believe that your opinions are really yours? Tell me where you were born, into what kind of family, what your parents did for a living, how many other children there were, what profession you are in, and a couple of other things, and I can pretty well tell you your opinions. So can anyone else who has done some research on this. This is because opinions are not a matter of thinking. We do very little *real* thinking—a lot of *having* thoughts, but that's not thinking.

We take everything personally—if the weather is bad, we take that personally. We think we are *doing* this thing that I am calling assessing, which leaves us with an illusion of control, as if we could stop assessing or stop voting. For example, "I make my own assessments, it is something I personally do—a personal phenomenon inside me—and I control it."

In fact, those assessments happen automatically. They walk in to work and meetings with us. We already know that we or other people are not good enough or committed enough. We already know how people are, how the project is, how the company is.

And it appears that we are personally "doing" that assessing and should stop. If you are personally doing that, then stop. Go ahead, try it. We are no more "doing" that than we are "doing" growing new cells or "doing" making our heart beat.

3. Already Knowing

A third dimension of our automatic listening, or a third fundamental filter that we listen through, is listening for what we already know, to have whatever is happening fit with what we already know. We listen in order to confirm what we already know. Have you ever found yourself responding to new information with thoughts such as "Oh, that's like Senge's 'Learning Organization'" or "that's like Prahalad's 'Strategic Intent'"— instantly relating what you hear to what you already know.

We automatically listen for and are an antenna for fit and confirmation. We agree with what fits, and we write off what does not fit. We have, at best, a two-minute window for what doesn't fit. We have almost no tolerance for not knowing, not understanding, not having the answer. We want to know, What is it? What is the definition? What is it good for? How do I do it? What can I use it for? and What will I get out of it?

231

Once we have these answers and explanations, we understand. We don't have to wonder about or inquire into what is possible. This is now a closed case. No more possibility—we've got our answers, never noticing that it is what we already know that is suffocating us. *We will never fit new possibilities into what we already know!*

> A top salesperson in a large department store was in a training program on new sales techniques. As she was listening to the trainer, she found herself saying, "This will never work. I know how to sell. You can't approach a customer like that. If you did, it would take all day to wait on one customer." Despite overwhelming evidence that the technique worked, she heard herself dismissing the possibility over and over again. The good news is that each time she caught this automatic listening, she was able to hear possibility in what was being said and to listen with real power. She reported later that she was amazed at the increased sales that she had almost missed.

We pretend to listen openly, but our "listening" is not a clean slate. We approach situations like this:

> I already know what sort of person I am, and I know what sort of person you are and what sort of people are on my team, and I know about this project, this field, this economy, this world—*now*, what is it you have to say?

We are conditioned to confirm what we know, and if something is said that does not fit, we will either disprove it or make it fit in some way. We don't decide to do this—it happens automatically, and our actions are determined by it. Here is what's interesting. We live as if it is all inside us. But what if it is not inside us but we are inside "it"—this automatic listening we have been examining? And that automatic listening or "superglue" determines your future; it is there before you even get there.

4. Looking Good

A fourth aspect that we listen for is, Is this safe? Am I going to look good? Is this going to promote my point of view, which I want to maintain?

We don't "think" that, and we don't consciously plan to listen that way. We don't even have to remember to listen that way—you and I are already organized to listen that way.

If you view yourself as a team player, as a leader, as open and candid, and then something happens that threatens that view, that threat must be "explained" away. We see ourselves in a particular way, and we do not want that disrupted. We are organized for maintaining the continuity of our view.

I recently asked a colleague, currently a vice-president at a Fortune 500 company, when he was going to be on the executive committee of his corporation. His immediate response was, "Not me! I could never do that." He was upset and annoyed—this did not fit with his view of himself.

Avoiding any disruption in our view of ourselves is not something that we consciously do; it is automatic. Yet this mode of "listening" determines our behavior. People would rather say nothing than risk saying the wrong thing. We are deeply concerned about being "right" and looking good. And we are committed to eliminating, avoiding, or explaining away anything that threatens our point of view. Given that no new possibilities will get through the filter, our career, our work life, and the future of our organization are seen against a background of resignation about the future. We don't have the freedom to create a new future. We are left with only a limited range of options, which are consistent with the past and, at best, an improvement over the past. That is not a future based in possibility; it is a future based in the past. In other words, no real possibility; only limited options.

5. Description

Our background listening says, "Work is a certain way, you are a certain way, the team, the project, the company, the field are a certain way." And we use language to talk about or describe it and label it "the way that it *already* is."

This is a fundamental paradigm: language is merely for labeling things that are already there; and, therefore, there is no power in talking, except to label things accurately or inaccurately. Work occurs as subject/object: there's you and other stuff that is already a certain way, which language represents. So we can *talk about* or describe work, the future, or a project, and we can talk about it correctly or incorrectly. We can put the right labels or the wrong labels on it, but there's no real possibility, no new thinking. Our work is set against a background of deep resignation regarding any real possibility.

All of this is designed to minimize risk. Our background listening is organized to already know and understand everything. It is designed to maintain conformity (including conforming by being a nonconformist). It is all already there, and it appears to us as fact, as truth.

This is an automatic mode of listening—we are not "thinking" this, it is "thinking" us—and it's not a personal problem. There is no real, authentic stepping out into the unknown.

6. Resignation

We go in to work as if today were just another version of yesterday and what will happen today were already known. We do not recognize this as resignation—we see it as being realistic, or worldly, or appropriately cynical.

We don't open our mouths and speak as if our speaking and listening would alter the project or the future. We open our mouths and talk, and others talk, but we are not expecting much to happen.

When I interview senior executives in a major company, I always know that I will find some men and women completely resigned about new possibilities for the future. These are good people, working hard, who really want to empower the vision and strategic intent of the corporation, but they are all working against a background of resignation. They have little belief that their speaking and listening can open up a whole new possibility for the company's future, the work being done, and the people doing the work. Rather, while they may be working hard, wanting great things to happen, they already know that "business as usual" will continue, and they adapt to and settle for that, resigned that there will be no new possibilities or breakthroughs.

It is important to begin to see that if you are resigned to the fact that work *is* a certain way and you *are* a certain way and other people *are* a certain way and your organization and division *are* a certain way, then all that's left is to adapt to "the way it is around here." All that is left is to settle for what is already so and listen for tips and techniques to improve it. It is even more important to see that we are resigned. That is what is given.

We are not an empty vessel, listening for what is actually happening, for what someone is saying, or for what is possible. We don't listen to conversation as it is; we hear selectively. Something is going on already, and we pretend that it isn't there. It is this mode of listening that acts as "superglue" and keeps an organization's culture locked in place.

When we are unaware of something, it controls us. Once we become aware, we have a say in the matter. The real power in this whole insight is to go beyond simply being aware of this and to "actively" catch yourself listening this way.

Here's the good news: if we have accomplished as much success and as many results as we have while being unaware of this "superglue," there is no telling what might be possible with the freedom given by recognizing it, including stepping beyond it.

Are you willing to take a chance on a real possibility? Are you willing to challenge the "given"? Are you willing to take on the possibility that you don't know how next week is going to go? Are you willing to sacrifice who you *know* you are for who you *could* be? If you are, then we could have a conversation that would determine how next week, next month, and next year are going to go. That is our invitation to the organizations and executives that we work with. Rather than finding the best adaptation to "business as usual," we ask, "What's possible? What's outside the predictable? What new future can we invent?"

The first step in generating a new future or creating a transformed organization is gaining the freedom to think in new ways. If we can see the design of the "superglue" and get it out into the light of day, the result will be an enormous freedom to hear what is actually being said, to listen in a new way, to recognize and identify the current culture or paradigm that is limiting us. This will give us the power to see, generate, and fulfill new possibilities, which will result in new futures.

Sabina A. Spencer is director of Eartheart Enterprises Inc., an international consulting company focusing on strategic leadership and change. She works with corporate clients throughout the world and prior to her current role spent eight years with the Exxon Corporation in England and Canada. Born in Ireland, she lived in England until she moved to the United States in 1985.

Spencer is a fellow of the World Business Academy and has served as visiting faculty member at a number of colleges and universities throughout the United States and England. She has written extensively about her work and is the author of *Reflections* (New York: Vantage Press, 1987) and coauthor of *Life Changes: Growing through Personal Transitions* (San Luis Obispo, Calif.: Impact Publishers, 1990). Her current work is focused on the changing nature of business in Europe and the development of global leadership consciousness.

15

Seven Keys to Conscious Leadership

Sabina A. Spencer

As a "new world" emerges, and many long-standing boundaries begin to disappear, we have an incredible opportunity to achieve new levels of human potential. The scientific model has led us to new ways of *seeing the world* and has also helped us to recognize its own limitations. In business, government, and society, we are being confronted with the results of depending heavily on a leadership style that is based on a reductionist view of reality.

The massive downsizing in organizations, the disenchantment in political systems throughout the world, and the increase in inner-city violence are all symptoms of this crisis in leadership. The challenge now is to change our "mind-set" to one that is more systemic in nature and to reclaim those aspects of human consciousness and compassion that many of us have denied in the service of such a scientific model.

If we look at traditional models of leadership, we find that they are often based on fear and separation with an assumption of "survival of the fittest." This orientation has fostered a leadership style that has been predominantly competitive, materialistic, territorial, and focused on the short term . This may have been entirely appropriate for our development as a species and our success as an industrial society, but it does not meet the needs of today's realities.

In a business strategy meeting of people drawn from many different functions of a U.S. research organization, the attendees had difficulty understanding why they were spending so much energy "fighting" over resources and competing with one another internally. They concluded that they had all colluded with the leadership team in promoting this internal tension and that if they were to be successful in their changing environment, they would have to challenge the existing culture, identify a common purpose, create a longer-term vision, share their resources, and learn to work more collaboratively. Lists like this are becoming commonplace as people question the appropriateness of their old ways of working together.

To meet the growing challenges, a new form of leadership is being heralded that is influencing the emergence of a global awareness in business and a sensitivity to the role of each of us in ensuring humanity's continued health and prosperity. It is a form of leadership that is more a state of consciousness than a set of skills or traits. It is in essence the birthright of everyone, not just the "select few."

Such a leadership consciousness recognizes the tremendous interdependency that exists not only among the departments and functions of an organization but among the nations of the world. This hopefully will ensure the future health and well-being of humanity as a whole by placing human dignity and environmental sensitivity in balance with the "rational" view.

Seven Keys

Conscious leadership finds its roots planted firmly in the earth. Its source is "divine" inspiration. It is not motivated by a desire to conquer and control. Its core values promote love and harmony in fostering a spirit of global cooperation. It is based on the assumption that if anyone loses, no one really wins, because, after all is said and done, there is no "us and them" anymore, just a growing awareness that we are all passengers on board what Buckminster Fuller referred to as "Spaceship Earth."

As I have explored the essence of this leadership orientation, seven keys have emerged from my doctoral research exploring the nature of global leadership. These are:

- Securing balance
- Generating passion
- Sharing power
- Inspiring love
- Voicing truth
- Living with purpose
- Honoring the mystery

In one way or another, these keys are already being seeded in organizations and are promoting an awareness of the role that each of us must play to ensure the continued health of not only the future of business but the future of our world.

Key #1: Securing Balance

Wherever I go these days, people seem to be talking about "balance." There's a growing awareness that things are out of balance not only in the broader ecological and economic sense but also in the way people are living their lives. In a recent meeting in Europe, a group of business executives talked about the need to create greater balance between their work and their family lives. They were feeling a great deal of stress because of the demands placed on them through their roles in the organization and their own personal needs for quality time with their loved ones.

All of them acknowledged that it was their personal lives that suffered and that, as a result, they were feeling some of the "hollowness" of success. Several of them described how they had achieved a great deal but still felt an absence of fulfillment, having lost touch with the spiritual aspects of their lives. They concluded that it was necessary to reevaluate their current life-styles, to identify their priorities in terms of securing a viable future for themselves and their families.

In meetings and workshops throughout the United States, businesspeople have been raising the issue of balance in relation to their own feelings of outer and inner security. As layoffs and downsizing increase, many are fearful that they will be unable to meet their basic needs for survival and safety. With the outer world continuing to change at an increasing rate, many are voicing the need to find a new kind of security inside them-selves. This "inner searching" is leading people in business to identify the importance of regaining balance in other areas of their lives and to recognize many of the social and economic imbalances that exist in the world.

In many respects, it is the pressure to redress these imbal-ances, both in people's everyday lives and in the world as a whole, that is a significant driving force in changing the nature of leadership in organizations. As we move forward, we need to create workplaces that balance the following:

1. Short- and long-term thinking

2. Local and global perspectives

3. The treatment of symptoms and the promotion of health

4. Enrichment of existing jobs and upward mobility

5. Teamwork and individual contribution

We also need to examine ways to establish greater equity in our organizational programs and processes so that everyone can feel both a sense of personal value and responsibility for the part they play in securing the future.

If, in the words of Black Elk (1972), we are to once more "walk in balance with the earth," we will each need to rediscover the meaning of balance in our own lives and reconnect to the part of ourselves that is the source of our own inner strength and stability. We will need to find new ways of meeting our needs for security and challenge the old assumptions that have placed such a strong value on the acquisition of and attachment to material goods.

Key # 2: Generating Passion

Only a few years ago, it was difficult to imagine people in organizations talking about the presence or absence of passion in their work. Yet today it is an issue that is frequently raised as people seek to rekindle the spark that comes from being able to express their own innate creativity in the workplace.

When people think about passion, it is usually in relation to sexual expression. In the world at large, it often comes from the union between two people; but in our work, *passion comes from our ability to use all of who we are in the expression of what we do.* Passion is a primary source of our creativity and has been the driving force behind many significant changes in human history. If channeled to serve both personal and organizational purposes, passion becomes the fuel for achieving extraordinary results.

People who are taking on the new leadership challenge tend to be passionate about what they do and experience an overall sense of well-being and self-confidence, whereas people who have lost the vitality that comes from being "turned on" to life feel a sense of apathy and self-doubt.

I have found that the secret to generating personal passion within organizations lies in our ability to truly value our own uniqueness and that of others, to accept the creative tension inherent in both our masculine and feminine forms of expression. For example, our ability to initiate action and to assert personal limits, as well as to support others' growth and be receptive to alternative points of view, helps to promote an environment where people feel safe to take risks and experiment with new ideas.

The pressure in the fifties and sixties for corporate conformity suppressed the creative potential of large numbers of people in the work force and promoted a more masculine orientation to work. Today, as we begin to acknowledge diver-

243

sity and place more women and minorities in leadership positions, we are beginning to develop organizational cultures that
honor differences, support creativity and, in the words of the
U.S. Army, encourage individuals to "be all that you can be"!

If securing balance forms the foundation for conscious
leadership then passion is the fuel to ignite the energy to begin
the process of transforming our personal and organizational
realities in the service of our global future.

Key #3: Sharing Power

Over the last decade, the term *empowerment* has become
widely used in companies throughout the world. On a trip to
Tokyo in early 1992, we found that many Japanese were curious
about the meaning of *empowerment* and how it was being used in
the Western world. From my own experience, it has value in
bringing the issue of power out onto the table, but it is also
adding to the confusion that already exists. In one of the many
corporations that have as a core value "an empowered work
force," it was interesting to hear an employee make the following statement: "So they want us to be empowered. Let's see if
they really mean it." This notion of "we and they" and "us and
them" is at the center of the issue of power.

In redefining power as a "key" to changing orientation to
leadership, I want to suggest that power and "will" provide the
energy to be self-determining and self-directing. If we lose or
"give away" our power, we are likely to feel frustrated and
"blocked" in what we do and who we are. Feelings of anger and
sadness often accompany a sense of powerlessness and, if
repressed, lead to low morale and low productivity in an organization. Accessing our personal power allows us to exercise
our will and to make choices that serve our own needs and the
needs of those around us and generates a vital energy in our
work.

When people have accepted their power to make a difference in ways that promote harmony and unity, they are also
unafraid to share their fears and their feelings of joy, anger, or
sadness, valuing them as rich sources of data. They support

openness and trust in the authentic expression of who they are. In so doing, they create a climate that encourages individuals to take risks, enjoy work, express creative potential, and generally experience a sense of high self-esteem while making a valuable contribution to the organization.

As feelings become more highly valued, there is greater sensitivity to this aspect of our humanness and more permission to be emotionally expressive. For instance, in many organizations that are going through major changes, forums are being created to allow that expression to take place with the help of a skilled facilitator.

In terms of a true sharing of power, we still have a very long way to go, and our fundamental assumptions will need to be continually challenged. The first steps are often the hardest to take, but I believe that some footprints have already been made. In the global arena, there is growing evidence of a changing orientation, and in many companies in Europe, it is becoming commonplace to hear people talking of sharing resources and promoting shared leadership in determining the collective future of the European Economic Community.

Key #4: Inspiring Love

The fourth key to conscious leadership takes us into an area that many refer to as the "softer side" of life. It is so called because of the difficulty we have in finding the language to describe exactly what we understand by words such as *inspiration* and *heart*. In the context of consciousness and leadership, these terms bring to mind the notion of compassion and nonviolence as well as a more spiritual orientation to work and life.

It is not uncommon these days to hear people in business talk about recapturing the "spirit" of the organization and describing how they are looking for new sources of inspiration. Some also talk about the need to be more loving toward one another and to be "open hearted." In the Consumer Products Division of AT&T, "love" is one of the core values of the business and operating culture. In an article in the division's newsletter, President Ken Bertacini stated, "Adding love to our Shared

Values challenges us to own our personal values of caring, trust, and respect. Certainly, these are all definitions of love. You can't care for someone, trust or respect them if you don't love them."

The nature of this kind of love goes beyond the quality experienced in interpersonal relationships into the area of unconditional love. Such love is not given or taken, nor is it used to illicit a certain response. It is more pervasive and becomes the root out of which all activity grows.

Many of us have been educated in ways that separate us from one another through the color of our skin, our race, our religion, our nationality, or our gender, often leading us to compete for scarce resources and superior status. There are winners and losers, and it is hard to be open with people, because they may not be trustworthy. If we look around the world today, we see that many global issues are rooted in this assumption of separateness and scarcity. It will take a significant shift in our basic beliefs for this to change.

Many of the most popular skill training and management development activities today are designed around the "softer" areas so that people can learn how to work together in ways that respect their differences and support a sense of unity of purpose. More attention is being given to building a supportive and nurturing climate in which people can develop and grow.

If we take a look at the core values of some of the major corporations in the world today, we see words such as *harmony, openness, trust, teamwork, balance, integrity,* and *respect for the dignity of every individual.* All of this suggests a desire to create a world of work that has in the words of educator Angeles Arrien "heart and meaning," where people bring to work not only their physical bodies but their whole being.

If we look into the future, I believe that we will see a stronger spirit of community emerging within our organizations. Corporate consultant Juanita Brown (1992) believes that the tradition of community "can serve to strengthen the performance of modern organizations, the individual lives and health of their members, and the fabric of the larger society within

246

which business finds its home." Such organizations will be characterized by the acceptance that continuous improvement, customer satisfaction, and bottom-line results depend greatly on the extent to which their members experience a sense of respect and personal well-being in an environment that values the "softer" aspects of our human nature and feels its connection to a larger "whole."

Key #5: Voicing Truth

Leadership without truth is like a tree with no roots—it will stand for a while, but as the winds of challenge and change begin to blow, it will fall as people learn that it has no living legitimacy. It is, unfortunately, not uncommon to hear people in business and other organizations describing how they don't believe what they're being told, or how "the management" says one thing and does another. The term "walking the talk" has become an everyday phrase and with the theme of "empowerment," people are being challenged more and more to model what they say they believe.

In a meeting in California, after hearing what they described as the "company line," the members of a corporation challenged their CEO to "tell us how it really is." After a pause, he accepted the challenge and began to describe his own view of the next few months. There was a tangible change in the energy of the group as they heard the "truth" about their company. People began to ask questions about what they could do; what the options were; whether there were some alternatives that hadn't yet been tried. The atmosphere changed from "Here we go again with the same old stuff!" to "Okay, so this is how it really is. What can we do?"

Needless to say, it was a powerful and uplifting meeting and set the tone for the attitude that was needed to see the company through the difficult times that lay ahead. In my experience, people really want to know the "truth" and are less afraid if they know it than if they believe that something is being hidden from them.

247

Yet it is sometimes hard for people to tell the truth, because our educational systems tell us *what* to think but in general fail to teach us *how* to think by using our own life's experience. The result is that many of us do not know our own "truth" and are not taught how to listen to our own inner voice that grows out of the silence.

Today, in companies all over the world, more emphasis is being put on finding ways to help us simply learn how to talk to one another. So often people speak from their *roles* and not from their *souls*. Even though they may have learned all the techniques, if the words are not connected to the deeper parts of themselves, others will find it hard to believe in what they say.

This whole area of "authentic" conversation is being emphasized and explored in many arenas. Physicist David Bohm (1980) has been spending the last few years exploring what he refers to as "dialogue." This involves people coming together not to "discuss" their opinions on an issue but rather to share their values and basic assumptions in order to seek deeper meaning and understanding of themselves and their colleagues. In so doing, they connect at a more profound level, developing a sense of compassion for their fellow human beings and recognizing the common bonds of their humanity.

Many decaying corporate cultures do not reward the truth. Sayings such as "they shoot the messenger around here" are commonplace. As those cultures are challenged and a different value set emerges, we must do all we can to help people "to be true to themselves" and provide the skills and relearning experiences necessary for everyone to "voice the truth" in ways that neither judge nor punish. It is only in the presence of truth that conscious leadership can emerge and genuine creativity and communication can come to life.

Key #6: Living with Purpose

As uncertainty about our collective future grows, many people are finding that they can no longer depend on the "outer world" to guide them through the turbulence and are therefore choosing to turn inward. In their search for more understanding and greater fulfillment, they are asking deeper questions of meaning. They are seeking to identify their life's purpose.

In many dinnertime conversations with men and women in business, and in executive coaching sessions, I have been surprised and delighted at the depth of their enquiry. Some are questioning not only the purpose of their own life and relationships but the purpose of their role and their organization's role in the future of the world.

In the past fifteen years, we have seen the notion of "vision" leaving the realm of the abstract and becoming a term that is used unhesitatingly in virtually every kind of organization. There are visioning retreats and examples of visionary leaders; there are short-term visions and long-term visions, vision statements, even vision buttons! But what is it that brings a vision statement to life and prevents it from lying dormant in a desk drawer or pinned to an office wall where no one sees it?

For a vision to be truly compelling and inspiring, it needs to be connected to a deeper sense of purpose that has meaning and value for everyone. Vision without a clear purpose will sometimes capture the minds but rarely the hearts of people.

The power of purpose in an organization lies in its ability to promote a sense of unity and shared direction, but only if its members can share in its creation and see how it also serves their sense of personal purpose. If this happens, then purpose provides the context for our passion and creativity to come to life, allowing us to enliven our minds and our spirits. By balancing our rational and intuitive abilities and accessing our imagination, we are able to reclaim many of the gifts that we left behind in childhood. In so doing, we can experience a sense of wonder at our own power to create new realities through our relationships and work.

In organizations that do not have a clear purpose, there frequently appears to be neither rhyme nor reason for many of the decisions that are made. Members of the organization find it hard to understand why they are having to cut costs when the profits are at an all-time high or why there is downsizing in one part of the company while there is recruiting in another. I have heard comments like "they don't know what they're doing from one day to the next."

With *purpose* as the guiding principle, every business decision must be made in terms of how it serves to further the purpose of the organization in the longer term and broader scope as well as in the shorter term and more local focus. Unfortunately, with our current Western business orientation, we are all too frequently sacrificing the future for the present. In so doing, we may make short-term gains, but the cost can be enormous in the long term.

Key #7: Honoring the Mystery

The seventh key to conscious leadership lies in the recognition that we live on the edge of our own discovery. We are at a point in our history where many of the old ways of working and managing don't work anymore. Our thinking is changing from a reductionist and mechanistic mind-set to one that is more systemic and acknowledging of the subjective experience of humankind. Our corporate structures are shifting from hierarchies to networks, and the world of business has already transcended national boundaries in creating a global economy.

These changes present each of us with an incredible opportunity to take a leadership role in creating a future that is different from the past. Leadership by its very nature suggests stepping into the unknown, charting new territories, and creating new realities. At this stage of our development, it appears that access to "new territories" lies in our ability to open our hearts and minds and journey into the deeper levels of human consciousness to discover new ways of thinking, behaving, and organizing.

All of this will take courage, commitment, and the belief that it is both possible and desirable for such a profound transformation to occur. As we're confronted with the growing global crises as well as a crisis of the human spirit, it would appear that there may not be an option. We have to find alternative ways of living and working together in this "new world" if we are to survive as a species.

The institution best placed to catalyze this transformation and to promote this changing consciousness is business. It is also in the context of business that people are beginning to find the freedom to ask questions about values and meaning. Organizations are actively encouraging their members to create new systems, share in the determination of the future, and reclaim their power to make a difference. More and more people are seeking to reunite the spiritual and rational aspects of their deeper humanity in order to find greater levels of fulfillment from their work.

It is an exciting time to be part of the changing world of business and to participate in the leadership that will take us into the next century. However, we must not fail to notice that there is also a great deal of fear that arises at a time of such significant change. This is most often rooted in the fear of stepping into the unknown and letting go of the familiar old patterns and beliefs that served us in the past. To minimize the impact of these changes, the six previous keys must be developed. By securing balance, generating passion, sharing power, inspiring love, voicing truth, and living with purpose, we will find it easier to trust our own inner knowing as we embrace the void that represents the unknown future.

It is through turning these keys that we gain new insights and realizations that allow us to trust beyond understanding, create deeper relationships, free ourselves from attachment, and achieve a sense of the power of our spiritual heritage. In business and through business, we must reconnect with the purpose and nature of work in the world and create productive and fulfilling environments.

To do this successfully requires a great deal of redefinition. We need to define what we mean by sustainable growth, economic health, and environmental sensitivity. These new definitions will need to be translated into activities and behaviors, and what better arena is there in the world today than that of business?

251

However, all of this also depends on a redefinition of leadership. And it has been my intention to suggest that the leadership of our collective future does not depend on a few people but rests on each one of us. The Seven Keys to Conscious Leadership open doorways into the potential that we each have to create a more loving world for ourselves and the generations to follow. Leadership is, in essence, everybody's business.

Conclusion

The Courage to Act

Pat Barrentine

It's one thing to read a collection of essays such as these and be inspired; it's quite another to know where to go from here.

It seems to me that above all else, the authors in this volume show us that profound change is overtaking every area of our lives and that the old ways of doing business don't have to rule any longer. They demonstrate that it is possible for us to create more humane and nourishing environments within the business setting, for men and women to work in a more even balance, and for feelings to have an appropriate role in the workplace.

Your challenge is to apply these ideas in your own life as the authors have. Almost without exception, the authors write of their personal journey, or inner quest, or spiritual evolution. Whatever the term one uses, it means doing the "inner work." If we are going to create a wholesome business environment, we have to enter into the endeavor as a complete person. For most of us that means being willing to look at our relationships—with parents, partners, children, friends, and co-workers. We have to be willing to heal the parts of our lives that don't work or that "get in our way." That's easy to say; it's another thing to do.

Being honest with ourselves is the first step. Use Barbara Fittipaldi's insights on automatic listening to assess your own ability to remain open to new information. Begin to develop your intuition by following the techniques offered by Mitani D'Antien. You will "quiet your mind," allowing new insights and ideas to come into your conscious awareness.

Whether you are a line worker, a supervisor, or a CEO, it's important to realize that whatever you do to be more whole will have a positive effect on your work. Top-down directives for change will not result in sustained organizational renewal. Individuals must lead the way. "New leaders" transform themselves before they can change their companies.

If you are inspired by the concepts presented in this book and want to introduce them into your workplace, it will require courage on your part. Not everyone is ready to look at life–or work—from a new perspective. Don't let that keep you from sharing yourself—what you are reading or what you have learned from your own search—with others. See yourself as a pioneer and move forward at a comfortable pace. Chances are you will find others who will support you but didn't have the tools or courage to initiate something on their own.

To help, you could create or join a support group of people who are willing to explore what it means to be "real" at work. If you feel too vulnerable sharing your innermost feelings with fellow workers, you might find the support outside the group with whom you work on a daily basis. On the other hand, support groups at work—based on exploring mutual interests, creating new opportunities in the company, sharing knowledge, developing skills—can also be life-changing, not only for the people involved, but for the company as well.

For some, it's not enough just to change their local home or work environment. Several of the authors in this book encourage us to broaden our perspective, to adopt a more global view. If you care deeply about a social, political, or environmental issue, support those organizations working for constructive change with your time, money, and knowledge.

If your main interest is business, join an organization focused on new ways of doing business. You will learn about several of these organizations by reading some of the publications listed in the Recommended Reading and References section of this book. In addition to books, we have included a list of periodicals, any one of which can give you continuing support and encouragement in your discovery process.

The great Native American leader Chief Seattle said it this way: "Man did not weave the web of life; he is merely a strand in it. Whatever he does to the web, he does to himself." I believe that what follows naturally from that statement is also the reverse: Whatever man does to himself, he does to the web. Whatever each of us does to become a more whole person affects the future of the human race.

May your journey be full of joy.

Pat Barrentine, editor

Recommended Reading, References and Resources

Books:

Aburdene, Patricia and John Naisbitt. *Megatrends for Women.* New York: Villard Books, 1992.

Assagioli, R. *Psychosynthesis.* New York: Penguin, 1976.

Argyris, Chris and D. Schon. *Organizational Learning: A Theory-in-Action Perspective.* Reading, Mass.: Addison-Wesley, 1978.

Arrien, Angeles. *The Four-Fold Way: The Paths of the Warrior, Teacher, Healer, and Visionary.* San Francisco: Harper, 1992.

Autry, James A. *Love and Profit: The Art of Caring Leadership.* New York: Morrow, 1991.

Bohm, David. *Wholeness and the Implicate Order.* London: Ark Paperbacks, 1980.

Breton, Denise and Christopher Largent. *The Soul of Economies: Spiritual Evolution Goes to the Marketplace.* Wilmington, Del.: Idea House Publishing Company, 1991.

Brown, Juanita. "Corporation As Community: A New Image for a New Era," *New Traditions in Business.* Ed. John Renesch. San Francisco: Berrett-Koehler, 1992.

Burlingham, Bo. "This Woman Has Changed Business Forever," *Inc.* magazine. June 1990, page 13.

Butruille, Susan G. "Corporate Caretaking," *Training and Development Journal*, April 1990.

Chandler, Alfred D. Jr. *Strategy and Structure: Chapters in the History of the Industrial Enterprise.* Cambridge, Mass.: MIT Press, 1962.

"Children in Crisis: A Special Report." *Fortune*, August 1992.

Coleman, D., Paul Kaufman, and Michael Ray. *The Creative Spirit: Companion to the PBS Television Series.* New York: Penguin Books, 1992.

DePree, Max. *Leadership Is an Art.* East Lansing: Michigan State University Press, 1987.

Dumaine, Brian. "Creating a New Company Culture," *Fortune.* January, 1990.

Eisler, Riane. *The Chalice & the Blade: Our History, Our Future.* New York: Harper & Row, 1988.

Eisler, Riane and David Loye. *The Partnership Way.* New York: HarperCollins, 1991.

Fassel, Diane. *Working Ourselves to Death.* New York: HarperCollins, 1990.

Fassel, Diane and Anne W. Schaef. *The Addictive Organization.* New York: HarperCollins, 1988.

Fisher, R., B. Patton, and W. Ury. *Getting to Yes.* New York: Houghton Mifflin, 1991.

Gallagher, Blanche, Ed. *Meditations with Teilhard De Chardin.* Santa Fe, N.Mex.: Bear and Co., 1988.

Gerber, Richard, M.D. *Vibrational Medicine: New Choices for Healing Ourselves.* Santa Fe, N.Mex.: Bear & Co., 1988.

Gilligan, Carol. *In a Different Voice: Psychological Theory and Women's Development.* Cambridge, Mass.: Harvard University Press, 1982.

Gleick, James. *Chaos.* New York: Viking Penguin, 1987.

Grof, Christina and Stanislav. *The Stormy Search for the Self.* Los Angeles: Jeremy Tarcher, 1990.

Greenwell, Bonnie. *Energies of Transformation: A Guide to the Kundalini Process.* Cupertino, Calif.: Shakti River Press, 1990.

Haessly, Jacqueline. *Peacemaking: Family Activities for Justice and Peace.* New York: Paulist Press, 1980.

Haessly, Jacqueline. *Learning to Live Together.* San Jose, Calif.: Resource Publications, 1989.

Harman, Willis. *Global Mind Change.* Indianapolis, Ind.: Knowledge Systems, Inc., 1987.

Harman, Willis. "21st Century Business: A Background for Dialogue," *New Traditions in Business.* Ed. John Renesch. San Francisco: Berrett-Koehler, 1992.

Harman, Willis and John Hormann. *Creative Work: The Constructive Role of Business in a Transforming Society.* Indianapolis, Ind.: Knowledge Systems, Inc., 1990.

Havel, Vaclav. *Open Letters. Selected Writings 1965-1990.* New York: Vintage Books, a division of Random House, 1991.

Helgesen, Sally. *The Female Advantage: Women's Ways of Leadership.* New York: Doubleday, 1990.

Henderson, Hazel. *Redefining Wealth and Progress: New Ways to Measure Economic, Societal, and Environmental Change.* Indianapolis, Ind.: Knowledge Systems, Inc., 1990.

Henderson, Hazel. *Paradigms in Progress: Life Beyond Economics.* Indianapolis, Ind.: Knowledge Systems, Inc., 1991.

Johnson, R. *Femininity Lost and Regained.* New York: Harper & Row, 1990.

Johnson, R. *Inner Work.* San Francisco: Harper & Row, 1986.

Jordan, Judith V., and others. *Women's Growth in Connection: Writings from the Stone Center.* New York: Guilford Press, 1991.

Jung, Carl G. *Memories, Dreams, Reflections.* Ed. Aniela Jaffe. New York: Pantheon Books, 1961.

259

Jung, Carl G. *Collected Works of C. G. Jung.* Vol. 6, Psychological Types. Bollingen Series, No. 20. Princeton, N.J.: Princeton University Press, 1971.

Korten, David C. *Getting to the 21st Century: Voluntary Action and the Global Agenda.* West Hartford, Conn.: Kumarian Press, 1990.

Land, George and Beth Jarman. *Breakpoint and Beyond.* San Francisco: HarperBusiness, 1992.

Lundin, William and Kathleen. *The Healing Manager: How to Build Quality Relationships & Productive Cultures at Work.* San Francisco: Berrett-Koehler, 1993.

Mack, Alice. *Beyond Turmoil: A Guide to Renewal Through Deep Personal Change.* Tuscon, Ariz.: Connexions Unlimited, 1992.

Mander, Jerry. *In the Absence of the Sacred: The Failure of Technology and the Survival of the Indian Nations.* San Francisco: Sierra Club Books, 1991.

McMillen, Kim. "Creativity and the Law," *The Colorado Lawyer.* Vol. 20, No. 6, 1991.

McMillen, Kim. "Good Communications Support Effectiveness, Empowerment, and Organizational Well-Being," *The New Leaders.* San Francisco: September/October 1992.

Mendlowitz, Saul, Ed. *On the Creation of a Just World Order.* New York: The Free Press, 1975.

Mische, Gerald. "The Debt Bomb," *Breakthrough.* Global Education Associates, Fall, 1988.

Mische, Gerald and Patricia. *Toward a Human World Order.* New York: Paulist Press, 1977.

Mische, Patricia. "Economics for the Planet," *Breakthrough.* Global Education Associates, Fall 1988.

Mische, Patricia. "Economics in an Interdependent World," *Breakthrough.* Vol. 10, No. 1, Summer/Fall, 1988.

Moore, Thomas. *Care of the Soul: A Guide for Cultivating Depth and Sacredness.* New York: HarperCollins, 1992.

Moss, Richard, M.D. *The Black Butterfly: An Invitation to Radical Aliveness*. Berkeley, Calif.: Celestial Arts, 1986.

Neihardt, John G. *Black Elk Speaks*. New York: Washington Square Press, 1972.

Nelson, J. *Healing the Split: Madness or Transcendence*. Los Angeles: Jeremy Tarcher, 1990.

Oakley, Ed and Doug Krug. *Enlightened Leadership*. Denver: Stonetree Publishing, 1992.

Ornstein, Robert, and Paul Ehrlich. *New World New Mind: Moving Toward Conscious Evolution*. New York: Doubleday, 1989.

Österberg, Rolf. *Corporate Renaissance: Business as an Adventure in Human Development*. Mill Valley, Calif.: Nataraj Publishing, 1993.

Ozaniec, Naomi. *The Elements of the Chakras*. Great Britain: Element Books Limited, 1990.

Parry, Danaan. "The Fear of Transformation," *Warriors of the Heart*. Cooperstown, NY: Sunstone Publishing, 1991.

Peck, M. Scott, M.D. *The Road Less Traveled*. New York: Simon and Schuster, 1978.

Peck, M. Scott, M.D. *The Different Drum: Community Making and Peace*. New York: Simon & Schuster, 1987.

Petersen-Lowary, Shiela. *The 5th Dimension: Channels to a New Reality*. New York: Simon & Schuster, 1988.

Ray, Michael and Alan Rinzler, Eds. *The New Paradigm in Business*. New York: Tarcher/Perigee, 1993.

Renesch, John, Ed. *New Traditions in Business: Spirit and Leadership in the 21st Century*. San Francisco: Berrett-Koehler, 1992.

Riley, M. *Corporate Healing*. Deerfield Beach, Fla.: Health Communications, Inc., 1990.

Russell, Peter. *The While Hole in Time*. San Francisco: Harper, 1992.

261

Russo, Clement L. "Productivity Overview: Recognizing the Human Dimension," *ReVision*. Winter '84/Spring '85, pages 68-73, page 73.

Sannella, L. *The Kundalini Experience: Psychosis or Transcendence?* Lower Lake, Calif.: Integral Publishing, 1987.

Sargent, Alice, and Ronald Stupak. "The Androgynous Manager." *Training and Development Journal*, 1989.

Schell, Jonathan. *Fate of the Earth*. New York: Alfred A. Knoph, 1982.

Schmookler, Andrew. *Fools Gold: The Fate of Values in a World of Goods*. San Francisco: Harper, 1993.

Schumacher, E. F. *Small is Beautiful: Economics as if People Mattered*. New York: Harper Torchbooks, 1973.

Sen, Gita. *Development, Crisis and Alternative Visions: Third World Women's Perspectives*. New Delhi, India: DAWN Secretariat, Institute of Social Studies Trust, 1985.

Senge, Peter M. *The Fifth Discipline: The Art and Practice of the Learning Organization*. New York: Doubleday, 1990.

Silker, Gretchen. *Multiple Mind: Healing the Split in Psyche*. Boston-London: Shambhala, 1992.

St. Romain, P. *Kundalini Energy & Christian Spirituality*. New York: Crossroad, 1991.

Tung, Rosalie. "Why American Managers are Failing Overseas." *UWM Research Journal*. Fall 1988.

Wheatley, Margaret J. *Leadership and the New Science: Learning About Organizations from an Orderly Universe*. San Francisco: Berrett-Koehler, 1992.

Business Periodicals*

At Work: Stories of Tomorrow's Workplace (bimonthly newsletter)
To subscribe, contact: Berrett-Koehler Publishers, Inc.
155 Montgomery St.
San Francisco, Ca 94104-4109
800-929-2929
Reg. rate: $75/1 year

Business Ethics: The Magazine of Socially Responsible Business
(bimonthly magazine)
To subscribe, contact: Mavis Publications, Inc.
52 South 10th St., #110
Minneapolis, MN 55403-2001
612-962-4700
Reg. Rate: $49/1 year
Free samples available

The New Leaders: The Business Newsletter for Transformative Leadership
(bimontly newsletter)
To subscribe, contact: New Leaders Press
2115 Fourth St.
Berkeley, CA 94710
800-959-1059
Reg. rate: $140/year, $260/2 years
Special rate: $98/year, $177/2 years

World Business Academy Perspectives (quarterly journal)
To subscribe, contact: Berrett-Koehler Publishers, Inc.
155 Montgomery St.
San Francisco, CA 94104-4109
800-929-2929
Reg. rate: $96/1 year

The Systems Thinker (newsletter, 10x/year)
To subscribe, contact: Pegasus Communications, Inc.
P. O. Box 120
Kendall Square
Cambridge, MA 02142
617-576-1231
Reg. rate: $167/ 1 year, $334/2 years
Special rate: $117/1 year, $197/2 year

*For international orders, check with publishers for extra shipping costs.

How to Contact Authors

Pat Barrentine, Director
Barrentine Associates
18037 Chaparral Drive
Penn Valley, CA 95946
916-432-3165

Jeanne Borei
515 Boulder Place
Signal Mountain, TN 37377
615-886-5230

Mitani D'Antien, Ph.D.
The D'Antien Center
P. O. Box 926
Fairfax, CA 94930

Riane Eisler
Center for Partnership Studies
P. O. Box 51936
Pacific Grove, CA 93950

Barbara Fittipaldi
Landmark Consulting
155 W. Main St., Box 996
Somerville, NJ 08876
908-722-5100

Carol Frenier
The Advantage Group
RR1, Box 119
Chelsea, VT 05038
802-889-3511

Jacqueline Haessly
Peacemaking Associates
2437 North Grant Blvd., Suite 2
Milwaukee, WI 53210
414-445-9736

Cheryl Harrison, President
Harrison Design Group
665 Chestnut Street, 3rd Floor
San Francisco, CA 94133
415-928-6100

Kathleen Keating, COO
Axion Design, Inc.
Box 629
San Anselmo, CA 94979
415-258-6800

Marie Kerpan, Vice President
Drake Beam Morin, Inc.
4 Embarcadero, Suite 650
San Francisco, CA 94111
415-765-5408

Kim McMillen
2344 - 19th Street
Boulder, CO 80304
303-440-8613

Jan Nickerson, Founder
Business Transformation Assoc.
222 Old Conn Path
Wayland, MA 01778
508-358-7247

Anne L. Rarich, President
Learning Exchange
315 College Road
Concord, MA 01742
508-369-9071

Barbara Shipka
4600 Colfax Ave. So.
Minneapolis, MN 55409
612-827-3006

Sabina Spencer, Director
Eartheart Enterprises, Inc.
84 Camino de Herrera
San Anselmo, CA 94960
415-258-0367

Hope Xaviermineo
P. O. Box 804
Glen Ellen, CA 95442
707-939-1406

Index

Aburdene, Patricia, 1
Abuse: and quality of life, 179-80, 187; tolerance of, 181-82
Addams, Jane, 119
Addictions, 181
Administrative system: centralized, 200-201; in pyramid organization, 197-98, 200
Advanced Intuition Training for Professionals, 215
Advertising, 85
Africa, relief work in, 89-93, 100-101
Agrarian values, 65-66
Androgynous Manager, The (Sargent, Stupak), 37
Aquino, Corazon, 28
Arrien, Angeles, 246
AT&T, 245-46
Authenticity: as cause of relationship, 94-95, 102; in community, 165, 169, 184; in conversation, 248; and power, 245; as a standard, 82-83; women's need for, 11-12, 16-17
Automatic listening: assessments in, 228-30; assumptions and, 227; confirmation in, 231-32; definition of, 226; description/labeling in, 234; dimensions of, 227-35; examples of, 225, 226; gaining awareness of,

235-36, 254; radar metaphor for, 228; resignation in, 234-35; self image in, 233
Autonomy, 52-53

Baby boomers: changing careers of, 81; disenchantment of, 79
Balance: and conscious leadership, 241-43; ecological, 122-23, 242-43; economic, 124-25; within global community, 69, 73-86, 121-28, 240; between inner and outer searching, 242; between personal and professional lives, 185, 241-42; in roles, 13, 64-65; and spiritual development, 13-14; standards for, 74; in values, 13; in workplace, 242
Barrentine, Pat, 9, 253
Bertacini, Ken, 245-46
Big Three auto makers, 5
Black Elk, 242
Blaming, versus taking responsibility, 51, 80-81, 155, 184
Body Shop International,The, 39, 129
Borei, Jeanne, 17, 133, 134, 165
Bottom line, 45, 174, 186
Brainstorming techniques, 20
Breakdown, global, 183-84. *See also* Crisis

Love: and conscious leadership, 245-
47; drive toward, 44-45, 51-52;
fears about, 52; unconditional,
246; in workplace, 23, 54-53, 245-
46
Loyalty Management Group, Inc.,
149

Macaca fusteuta, 188-89
McMillen, Kim, 14, 69, 70, 105
Management: balanced with visionary
leadership, 64-65, 68; creative use
of resources in, 57-58; and
honoring uniqueness, 60-61, 68;
and rebuilding organization, 58-
60. *See also* Managers
Management models: competitive,
239-40; dominator, 12, 28-29;
gardening, 55-68; hierarchical/
military, 3-5; kinetic circle, 202-
207; mushroom, 56; partnership,
12, 35-40; pyramid, 197-98, 200,
201; web style, 5, 37-38. *See also*
Dominator model; Partnership
model
Managers: and community-building
process, 172-74; "community
circle" meetings of, 173; healing
the isolation of, 220-21; toward
partnership model of, 38-39; role
of, in dominator society, 29, 38;
nurturing by, 63-64, 68; reciprocal
responsibility of, 155; self-
aggrandizement of, 77; women as,
37-38. *See also* Leadership;
Management; Senior executives
Masculine: versus feminine energy,
137; and power, 28-29; qualities
of, 38-39; as social construct, 23,
30-31. *See also* Gender roles
Meacham, Colquitt, 43
Media, truth in, 82-83
Meetings, strategy: decision-making
style in, 20
Men: changes in attitudes of, 38;
competition in, 83; decision-

making styles of, 48-49; frustration
of, with corporate environment, 10;
moral development of, 48, 49;
partnership of women with, 12, 38-
39, 40; perspectives of, 20-21;
trusting own judgment of, 48. *See
also* Masculine
Mendlowitz, Saul, 121
Merton, Thomas, 116
"Metanoia," 107
Mind-set change, 160, 239, 250
Mindmapping, 143-44
Minoan society, 33-34
Minorities, and representative leadership,
77-78, 244
Miracle making, through commitment to
vision, 177-79
Mische, Patricia, 124
Moral development, of women versus
men, 48, 49
Morale, in workplace, 174
Murray, W. H., 178
Mushroom theory, 56
Mystery, honoring the, 250

Naisbitt, John, 1
Networks: versus community, 17; among
company core groups, 134, 157-59;
for job search, 15-16, 134, 142, 146-
47; mindmapping for, 143-44; "old
boys'," 16; versus support groups, 15;
in times of transition, 16; of women
employees, 158-59
New Traditions in Business (Harman),
211
Nickerson, Jan, 15-16, 133, 134
Nurturing: by management, 27, 63-64; in
workplace, 10, 23, 30, 38, 109, 115

Oligarchy, 84
Openness, 18-20; in work relationships,
193
Organizational culture: examination of,
224-25; resignation to usual, 234-35;
unexamined assumptions in, 223,
224, 227. *See also* Automatic

273